The KDP Blueprint

Step-by-Step to Publishing Your book

Northport Booksellers Spring Farm
NSW Australia 2570

The KDP Blueprint/ José F. Nodar. -- 1st ed.

ISBN 978-1-7637054-8-7 - Paperback

ISBN 978-1-7637054-9-4 - E-book

Table of Contents

Dedication

To my wife Miriam, who has supported me in every step of the way. I love you heaps, my muse!

To my daughter and stepdaughters, who have put up with all my mistakes and suffered through all my horrible jokes.

Additionally, I extend my gratitude to my grandchildren and step-grandchild for enduring my quirks and eccentricities throughout the years.

And I special thank you to my friends who have patiently listened to my endless chatter about my writing endeavours.

To my fellow partners in crime, authors in the family of Camden Books and Quick Story Tales who have supported me in so many ways. I am forever grateful for your trust and friendship.

Could not have done with without the help of my copyeditor/ proofreader, book cover designer and my audiobook narrators. Thank you for making me look good!

Finally, my heartfelt thanks to the wonderful readers that have purchased my books in the past and I hope will continue to do so in the future.

It's all for you.

Module 1

Unlocking The Potential Of Book Creation With Ai

Creating and publishing a book has never been more accessible. With the rise of artificial intelligence and self-publishing platforms like Amazon Kindle Direct Publishing (KDP), the barriers that once stood in the way of becoming an author have disappeared. You now have the tools to turn your ideas into a reality and share them with readers around the world.

This journey begins by understanding why self-publishing is a powerful opportunity, how AI can simplify the process, and which resources will help you get started.

The Game-Changing Power of Self-Publishing

Self-publishing has transformed the way stories, ideas, and expertise are shared. No longer do you need the approval of traditional publishing houses, wait through months of submissions, or face rejections. Now, anyone with determination and creativity can write, publish, and sell a book to a global audience.

Why Self-Publishing is a Powerful Opportunity:

1. **Creative Freedom**: Every decision, from the content to the design, is entirely under your control. You decide how your book looks, what it says, and how it connects with readers.

2. **Easy Access**: The path to publishing is no longer limited to professional authors. If you have an internet connection and an idea, you can publish a book.

3. **Better Earnings**: Unlike traditional publishing, where royalties are often low, platforms like Amazon offer up to 70% royalties, allowing you to keep more of what you earn.

4. **Reach Readers Worldwide**: Your book becomes instantly accessible to readers around the globe, whether they are browsing on their Kindle or looking for a paperback.

5. **Build Passive Income**: Once published, your book can generate income for years without additional effort, creating a steady revenue stream.

How Artificial Intelligence Simplifies the Process

Artificial intelligence tools like ChatGPT have made creating and publishing books easier and faster than ever. Whether you're an experienced writer or someone who struggles to get started, AI can assist at every stage of the process.

Key Ways AI Can Help:

1. **Generating Ideas**: AI can help you brainstorm book topics, titles, and even chapter outlines. If you need help to figure out where to start, AI can provide fresh and marketable ideas.

Prompt Example: *"Suggest five book topics that would appeal to beginners in personal finance."*

1. **Structuring Your Book**: AI can create detailed chapter outlines in seconds, giving you a roadmap to follow as you write.

Prompt Example: *"Create a chapter outline for a book on productivity for busy professionals."*

1. **Drafting Content**: AI can help you write engaging introductions, expand on ideas, and develop content for each chapter. It's like having a writing assistant available 24/7.

2. **Editing and Refining**: Tools like Grammarly can help polish your content, ensuring it is error-free, clear, and professional.

3. **Saving Time**: Tasks that once took weeks can now be completed in hours. With AI, you can focus on creativity while the technology handles repetitive tasks.

Essential Tools for Book Creation and Publishing

Getting started requires the right tools. Here are the resources you'll need to create, design, and publish your book:

1. AI Platforms

- **ChatGPT**: This tool will help you brainstorm ideas, create outlines, and draft content. It's user-friendly and extremely powerful. https://chatgpt.com/
- **Grammarly**: Use this to edit your writing for grammar, spelling, and style.

2. Design Tools

- **Canva**: A versatile tool for creating professional-quality book covers and promotional materials. https://canva.com
- **MidJourney or DALL-E**: AI-powered platforms that generate unique and creative illustrations or visuals for your book cover.

3. Publishing Platform

- **Amazon KDP**: This is where your book will come to life. You can publish ebooks, paperbacks, and even hardcovers with ease. Visit kdp.amazon.com to get started.

4. Formatting Tools

- **Google Docs or Microsoft Word**: These tools are ideal for drafting and formatting your manuscript.
- **Adobe Acrobat**: Use this to convert your manuscript into a print-ready PDF format for paperbacks.

Let's Get Started: First Steps to Success

Creating a book begins with generating ideas and choosing a topic that resonates with readers. AI can be your best brainstorming partner at this stage.

Task 1: Generate Book Ideas

Use ChatGPT to brainstorm book topics by providing clear prompts:

Prompt Example: *"Suggest three book ideas in the self-help genre for beginners."*

Response Example:

1. "The Power of Small Steps: How to Achieve Big Goals by Starting Small,"
2. "Stress-Free Living: Simple Habits to Create a Balanced Life,"
3. "Mindset Mastery: Unlocking the Secrets to Confidence and Success,"

Task 2: Create a Chapter Outline

Once you've selected a topic, ask AI to help structure the book:

Prompt Example: *"Create a chapter outline for a book about staying motivated in fitness."*

Response Example:

1. The Importance of Setting Goals
2. Building a Routine That Works for You

3. Overcoming Mental Barriers
4. Staying Consistent During Life's Challenges
5. Celebrating Progress and Achievements

Save this outline,—it will serve as the roadmap for your manuscript.

Bringing Ideas to Life with AI

Once your topic and outline are ready, the next step is drafting your manuscript. AI can help you develop content for each chapter, ensuring your writing is engaging and informative.

Task 3: Write Your Introduction

Start by drafting an introduction that hooks readers and sets the tone for the rest of the book.

Prompt Example: "Write a 300-word introduction for a book titled 'Stress-Free Living: Simple Habits to Create a Balanced Life.'"

Response Example (Excerpt): "In a world filled with deadlines, responsibilities, and constant distractions, finding balance can feel impossible. This book is here to show you that a stress-free life is within reach. Through simple habits and actionable strategies, you'll learn how to prioritize what matters, eliminate unnecessary stressors, and create a life filled with calm and clarity..."

Building Momentum

With the foundation in place, you're ready to move forward. The tools and techniques outlined here will simplify the process, making it not just achievable, but enjoyable. By combining your creativity with AI's capabilities, you can craft a book that captivates readers and fulfils your vision.

Remember, every influential book begins with a single idea—and now you have the tools to bring that idea to life.

Module 2

Developing a Manuscript Using AI

The journey from an idea to a completed book begins with crafting a compelling manuscript. This step is often daunting, but artificial intelligence simplifies the process by acting as your brainstorming partner, writing assistant, and editor. You'll discover how to structure your book, generate engaging content, and refine your writing to create a polished manuscript that captures readers' attention.

Shaping Your Idea into a Clear Structure

Organizing your ideas into a logical flow is essential for creating a book that resonates with readers. A well-thought-out structure ensures your audience can follow your narrative or argument effortlessly. AI tools can help you map out your book's framework in minutes, eliminating guesswork and making the process enjoyable.

Start with Your Core Message

Ask yourself: What is the primary goal of this book? Whether it's educating, inspiring, or entertaining, the purpose will guide the direction of your content. Think about the audience's pain points or desires and how your book addresses them.

Example Prompt: *"Suggest a chapter structure for a book about boosting productivity for remote workers."*

AI Response:

1. Understanding the Challenges of Remote Work
2. Setting Up Your Ideal Workspace
3. Time Management Strategies for Maximum Efficiency
4. Overcoming Procrastination and Distractions
5. Balancing Work and Personal Life
6. Tools and Resources to Stay Productive

Expand Each Chapter with Subtopics

Each chapter needs depth to keep readers engaged. Break the content into smaller sections, making it easier to digest.

Example Prompt: *"Outline the key points for a chapter on time management for remote workers."*

AI Response:

- The importance of creating a daily schedule
- Using time-blocking techniques

- Prioritizing tasks with the Eisenhower Matrix
- Setting boundaries to avoid burnout
- Adapting to unexpected interruptions

With this framework, you have a roadmap to guide your writing process, ensuring that no critical points are overlooked.

Generating Content with ChatGPT

With your outline ready, it's time to transform it into engaging and valuable content. AI tools excel at generating drafts, offering examples, and helping you refine your writing.

Write Attention-Grabbing Introductions

Every chapter should begin with a strong introduction that sets the stage and hooks the reader. Use AI to craft these compelling openers.

Example Prompt: "Write an introduction for a chapter on overcoming procrastination for remote workers."

AI Response (Excerpt): "Procrastination is the silent killer of productivity. In the comfort of your home, distractions can quickly derail even the most focused individual. This chapter explores actionable strategies to overcome procrastination, build momentum, and achieve your goals with consistency..."

Expand Key Ideas with Examples and Explanations

Bring depth to your content by using AI to elaborate on your key points with relatable examples and actionable advice.

Example Prompt: *"Explain how the Eisenhower Matrix helps prioritize tasks."*

AI Response: "The Eisenhower Matrix categorises tasks based on urgency and importance. Tasks that are both important should be done immediately. Non-urgent but important tasks should be scheduled. Urgent but less important tasks can be delegated, and non-urgent, non-important tasks should be eliminated. This method helps remote workers focus on what truly matters, reducing overwhelm and increasing efficiency..."

Incorporate Real-Life Scenarios

Make your content relatable by weaving in real-life scenarios or hypothetical examples. This approach helps readers connect with the material and see its practical application.

Example Prompt: "Describe a scenario where time-blocking helped a remote worker improve their productivity."

AI Response: "Sarah, a graphic designer working remotely, struggled with meeting deadlines. By adopting time-blocking, she allocated specific hours for client projects, admin tasks, and creative breaks. This structure not only improved her focus but also left her evenings free for personal time..."

Polishing Your Manuscript

Even the best drafts need refinement. AI tools are invaluable for improving grammar, style, and overall readability, ensuring your manuscript is professional and reader-friendly.

Simplify and Clarify Your Writing

Use AI to refine complex sentences and enhance the flow between paragraphs. This ensures your ideas are communicated clearly.

Example Prompt: *"Rewrite this paragraph to make it concise and engaging: [Insert text]."*

Enhance Grammar and Style

Leverage tools like Grammarly or Hemingway Editor to catch errors and improve the overall quality of your writing. These tools ensure your tone is consistent and appropriate for your target audience.

https://www.grammarly.com/

https://hemingwayapp.com/

Add a Personal Touch

AI-generated text serves as a sound foundation, but your voice is what makes the manuscript unique. Add anecdotes, personal insights, or humour to establish a deeper connection with readers.

Creating Engaging Chapter Endings

A well-crafted conclusion leaves readers feeling satisfied and eager to continue. Use the end of each chapter to reinforce key points and motivate action.

Example Conclusion: *"Now that you understand the principles of time-blocking, take a moment to apply this technique to your daily schedule. Reflect on how it improves your focus and helps you accomplish your goals more effectively..."*

Incorporate reflection prompts actionable tasks or thought-provoking questions to maintain momentum.

Exercise: Draft Your First Chapter

Use these steps to create a fully developed chapter:

1. **Select a chapter**: Choose a topic from your outline that excites you.

2. **Draft an Introduction**: Use AI to generate an opening paragraph that hooks readers.

3. **Expand on Key Points**: Break down the chapter into sections using AI to fill in details, examples, and step-by-step instructions.

4. **Conclude Effectively**: Summarise the chapter and include a reflection prompt or action step.

Example Prompt: *"Write an opening paragraph and three main points for a chapter about building a productive home workspace."*

By completing this exercise, you'll have a comprehensive chapter ready to refine and incorporate into your manuscript.

Inspiring Confidence in Your Writing

AI makes writing approachable, even for those who feel uncertain about their skills. With the proper prompts and tools, you can transform your ideas into a cohesive and compelling manuscript. Developing your first chapter is a significant milestone, bringing you one step closer to a finished book that educates, inspires, or entertains.

Next, you'll discover how to enhance your book's visual appeal with a captivating cover design that captures attention and reflects your message.

Module 3

A Practical Example

It's time to put theory into practice by crafting a sample fitness book. This hands-on approach will show how to take an idea, structure it, and transform it into a compelling manuscript with ChatGPT. By walking through the creation of a beginner's fitness guide, you'll see how to apply these techniques to your project.

Go to ChatGPT.

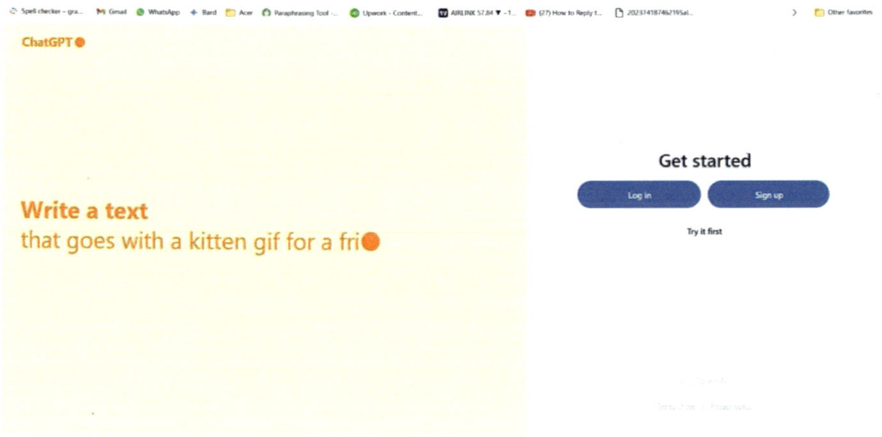

Next click Sign Up if you don't have an account or sign in if you already have. Enter the details as follows.

Or, you can continue with Google as well.

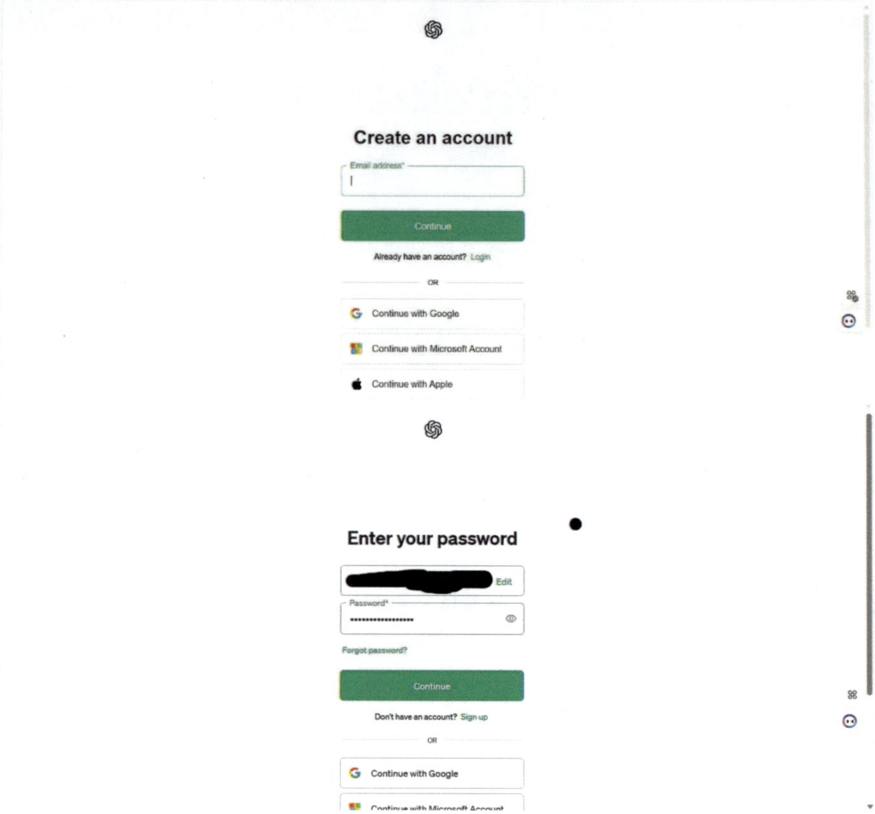

Once you added all the details, you will get this page.

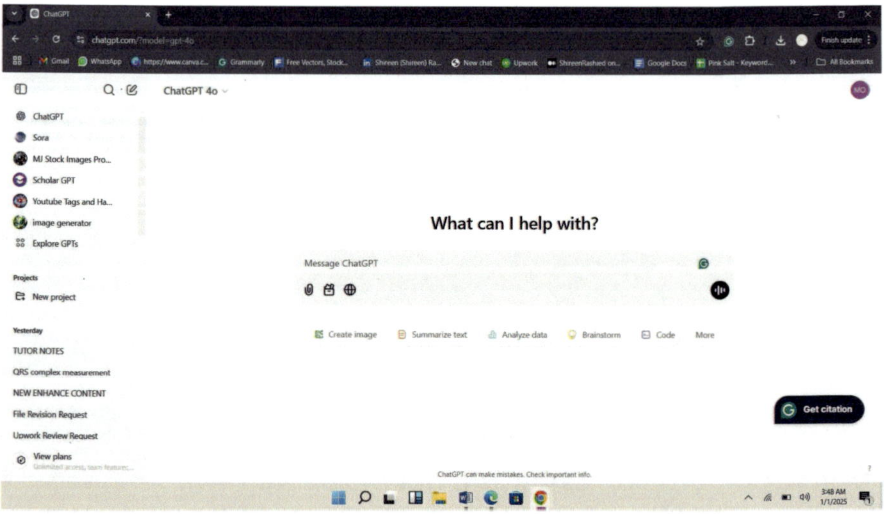

Start giving prompts and get the content for your book as follows.

Defining the Concept and Audience

Before writing a single word, clarity on your audience and concept is crucial. For this fitness book example, the target audience is beginners seeking an easy-to-follow guide to home workouts. This focus makes the content relatable and actionable for readers who want to start their fitness journey.

Steps to Define the Concept:

1. **Understand the Target Audience**:
   - Think about their goals and challenges. Beginners often want simple exercises, minimal equipment, and quick results.

Prompt Example: *"Suggest book topics for a fitness guide aimed at beginners."*

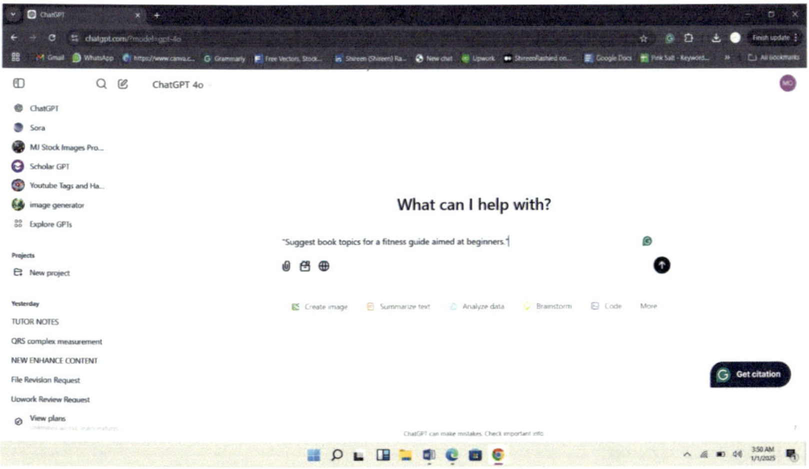

AI Response:

You will get the title as follows.

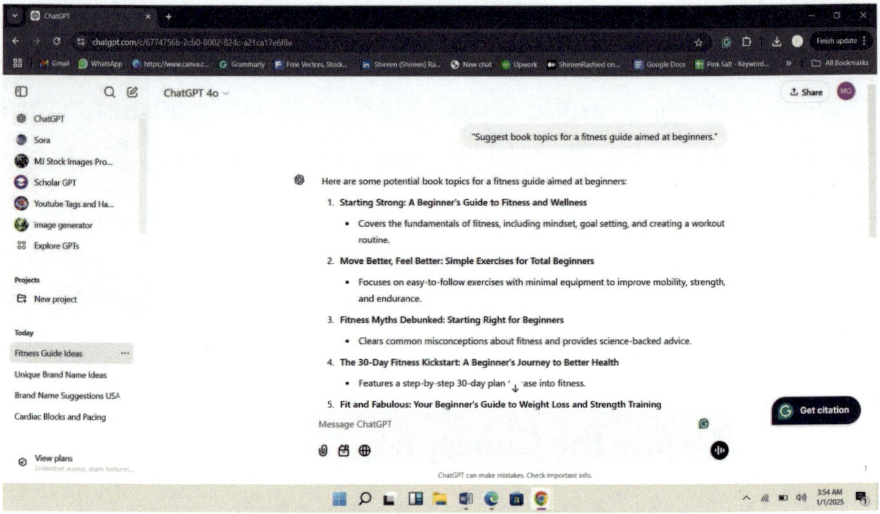

- **Starting Strong:** A Beginner's Guide to Fitness and Wellness
- **Move Better, Feel Better:** Simple Exercises for Total Beginners
- **Fitness Myths Debunked:** Starting Right for Beginners
- **The 30-Day Fitness Kickstart:** A Beginner's Journey to Better Health
- **Fit and Fabulous:** Your Beginner's Guide to Weight Loss and Strength Training
- **"Home Fitness:** A Beginner's Guide to Staying Active."

Building the Structure

Every outstanding book needs a clear and engaging outline. The chapters should flow logically, taking readers from understanding the basics to implementing the advice in their daily lives.

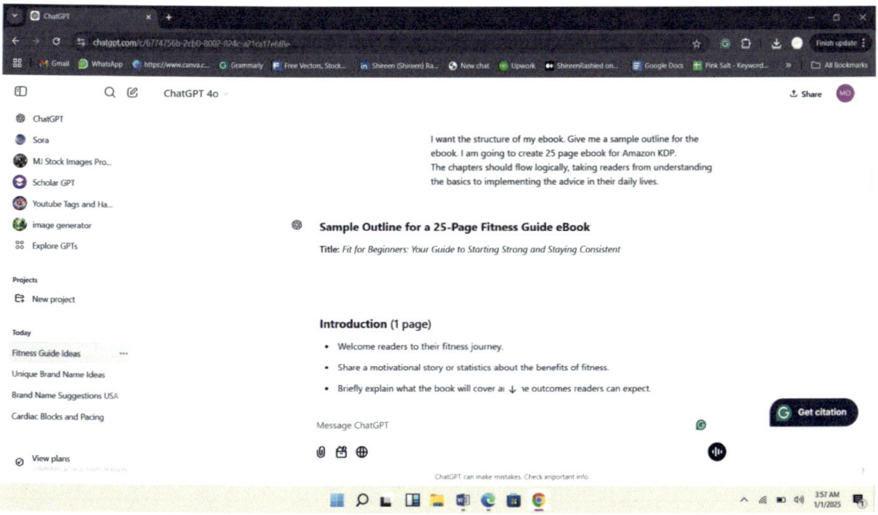

Example Outline for the Fitness Book:

Introduction

- Welcome readers to their fitness journey.
- Share a motivational story or statistics about the benefits of fitness.
- Briefly explain what the book will cover and the outcomes readers can expect.

Chapter 1: Why Fitness Matters

- Explain the physical, mental, and emotional benefits of fitness.
- Address common fears and misconceptions beginners face.
- Highlight how slight changes can lead to long-term results.

Chapter 2: Setting Goals that Stick

- Discuss the importance of realistic and specific fitness goals.
- Introduce the SMART goal framework (Specific, Measurable, Achievable, Relevant, Time-bound).
- Provide examples of beginner fitness goals (e.g., walk 5,000 steps daily, complete three workouts per week).

Chapter 3: Understanding the Basics of Fitness

- **Types of Fitness**: Cardio, strength training, flexibility, and balance.
- **Key Terms**: Reps, sets, heart rate zones, and rest days.
- **Common Equipment**: Resistance bands, dumbbells, yoga mats, and bodyweight exercises.

Chapter 4: Creating Your First Fitness Routine

- How to structure a beginner-friendly weekly workout schedule.
- A sample plan: 3 days of moderate exercise, 2 days of light activity, 2 rest days.
- Tips for staying consistent, including scheduling and tracking progress.

Chapter 5: The Role of Nutrition in Fitness

- Basics of balanced eating: macronutrients and micronutrients.
- Importance of hydration and timing meals around workouts.
- Simple tips for meal prepping and avoiding fad diets.

Chapter 6: Overcoming Common Challenges

- Address common roadblocks like lack of time, motivation, or energy.
- Tips for overcoming excuses and staying focused.
- Strategies for building a support system and celebrating small wins.

Chapter 7: Staying Safe and Injury-Free

- Importance of warming up and cooling down.
- Proper form for common exercises.
- When to rest and listen to your body.

Chapter 8: Tracking Progress and Staying Motivated

- How to track improvements (e.g., strength, endurance, measurements).
- Importance of non-scale victories, like increased energy and better sleep.
- Using fitness apps, journals, or simple logs to stay accountable.

Chapter 9: Making Fitness a Lifestyle

- Integrating movement into your daily routine.
- The importance of adaptability and trying new activities.
- Tips for maintaining fitness habits long-term.

Conclusion

- Reiterate key takeaways and motivate readers to take action.
- Share encouragement for sticking with the journey.
- Invite readers to connect via a social platform or website for further resources.

Quick Reference Guide

- A list of beginner exercises with illustrations or descriptions.
- A cheat sheet for healthy eating habits or workout templates.

Writing the Content

Once the structure is ready, each chapter can be expanded into detailed, engaging content. ChatGPT tools make this process smoother by providing well-crafted drafts and actionable advice.

Start writing content by giving prompts as follows.

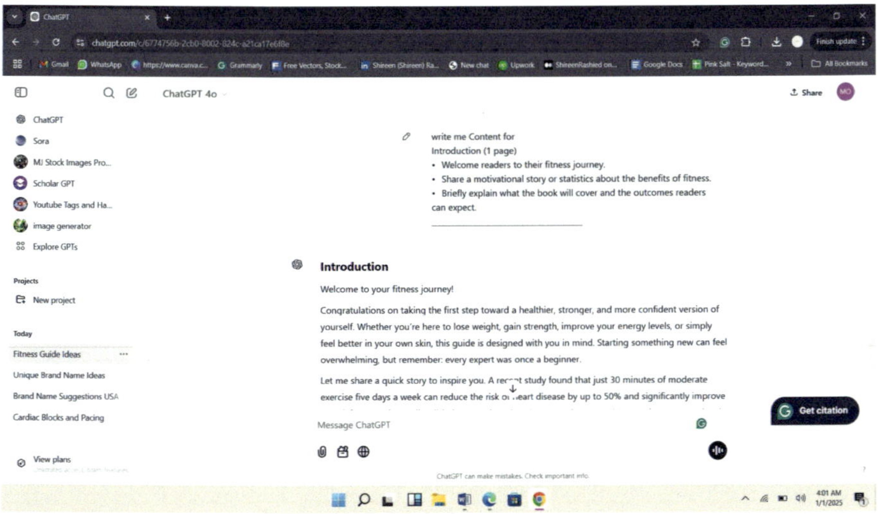

Introduction

Welcome to your fitness journey!

Congratulations on taking the first step toward a healthier, stronger, and more confident version of yourself. Whether you're here to lose weight, gain strength, improve your energy levels, or simply feel better in your own skin, this guide is designed with you in mind. Starting something new can feel overwhelming, but remember: every expert was once a beginner.

Let me share a quick story to inspire you. A recent study found that just 30 minutes of moderate exercise five days a week can reduce the risk of heart disease by up to 50% and significantly improve mood, focus, and overall well-being. Imagine what those 30 minutes could mean for you—not just in the short term, but for the rest of your life. Think of fitness as an investment in your future self, one small step at a time.

In this guide, we'll cover everything you need to know to start strong and stay consistent. You'll learn how to set achievable fitness goals, build an exercise routine that works for your schedule, and overcome common challenges like lack of motivation or time. We'll also touch on the role of nutrition, staying safe during workouts, and tracking your progress in meaningful ways.

By the end of this book, you'll have the tools, knowledge, and confidence to make fitness a lasting part of your lifestyle. Remember, you don't need to be perfect; you just need to start. Together, we'll make this journey both enjoyable and rewarding.

Let's take that first step together!

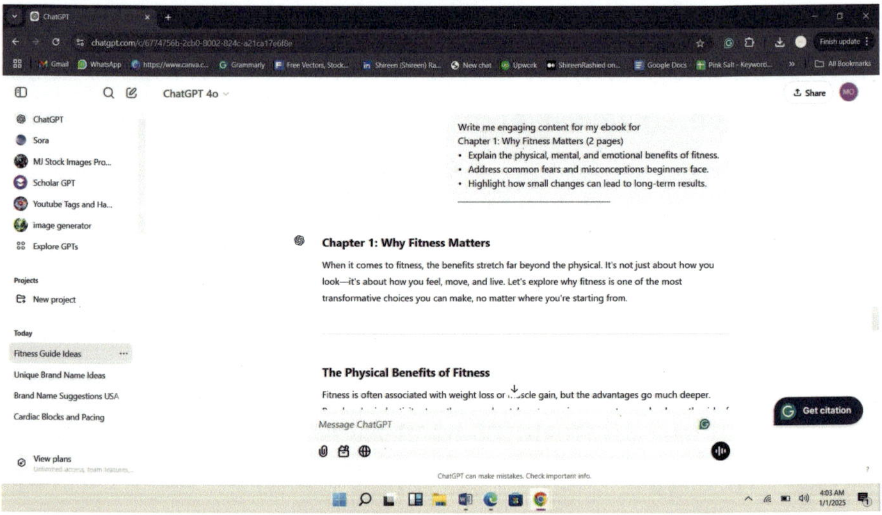

Creating Chapter Content:

AI/ChatGPT can help generate detailed explanations, exercise instructions, and tips for each chapter.

Generate content for the chapters as follows:

Response

Chapter 1: Why Fitness Matters

When it comes to fitness, the benefits stretch far beyond the physical. It's not just about how you look—it's about how you feel, move, and live. Let's explore why fitness is one of the most transformative choices you can make, no matter where you're starting from.

The Physical Benefits of Fitness

Fitness is often associated with weight loss or muscle gain, but the advantages go much deeper. Regular physical activity strengthens your heart, boosts your immune system, and reduces the risk of chronic conditions like diabetes, high blood pressure, and arthritis. It also improves flexibility, balance, and posture, reducing the likelihood of injuries in everyday life.

Even minor changes can make a difference. Studies show that walking just 20-30 minutes a day can lower the risk of cardiovascular disease and enhance your overall energy levels. Fitness doesn't mean hours in the gym—it's about finding movements that feel good for your body.

The Mental and Emotional Benefits

Fitness isn't just a workout for your body; it's a reset button for your mind. When you exercise, your brain releases endorphins, often referred to as "feel-good" hormones. These natural mood boosters help reduce stress, anxiety, and symptoms of depression, leaving you with a clearer mind and a more positive outlook.

Moreover, regular movement improves sleep quality, enhances focus, and even boosts memory. Imagine starting your day with more energy and mental clarity—fitness makes that possible. It's not about doing everything at once; it's about doing something that lifts your spirits and builds confidence over time.

Common Fears and Misconceptions

Let's address the elephant in the room. Many beginners worry about being judged, failing, or not knowing what to do. It's normal to feel this way, but remember: fitness is a personal journey, not a competition. Everyone starts somewhere, and most people are far more focused on their own goals than on judging yours.

Another common misconception is that fitness requires drastic lifestyle changes or expensive equipment. In reality, small, consistent actions—like taking the stairs, stretching in the morning, or following a 10-minute workout video—can have a profound impact over time. You don't need to overhaul your life overnight. Think progress, not perfection.

Slight Changes, Big Results

The beauty of fitness lies in its simplicity. Small, consistent steps build momentum, and that momentum transforms into long-term results. Start with one achievable goal, such as walking more, drinking enough water, or dedicating 15 minutes to stretching. These minor victories fuel your confidence and motivate you to keep going.

Remember, fitness is about what you gain—not what you lose. It's the energy to play with your kids, the strength to carry groceries without strain, and the mental resilience to tackle life's challenges. By embracing fitness, you're choosing to invest in a healthier, happier, and more vibrant future.

Fitness matters because *you* matter. It's not about perfection or comparison; it's about becoming the best version of yourself, one step at a time. With each slight change, you're not just changing your body—you're transforming your life.

Let's start small, dream big, and take this journey together.

Generate content for all the remaining chapters in the same manner.

After generating the content, we will format it in word document as follows.

Make sure your margin measurement settings are set to inches instead of cm, you can do that by following this tutorial:https://support.microsoft.com/en-us/office/change-units-used-for-margin-measurement-c65a06a7-2555-45d2-8912-f33c7e6fa404#ID0EBBD=Newer_Windows_versions

Then follow those steps below

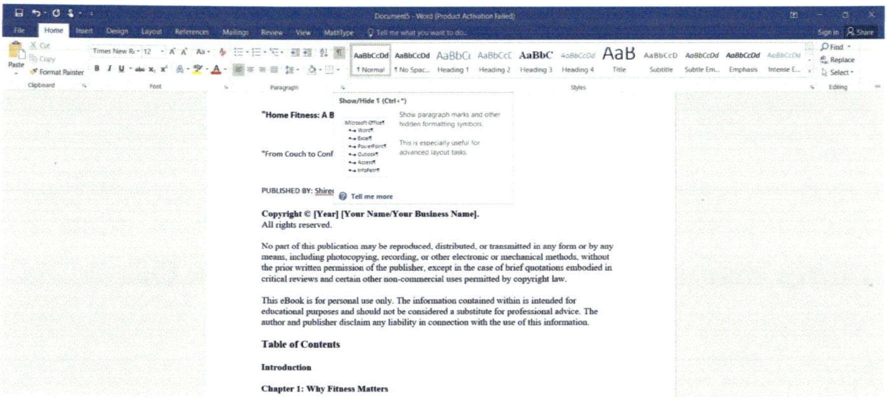

Select All and change the text to your desired font.

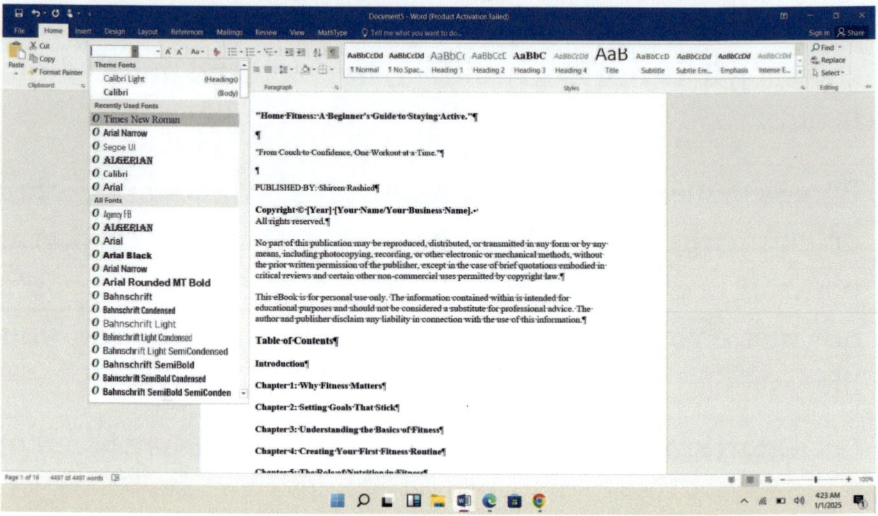

Next, go to layout > page setup and change size to 6x9 (custom size)

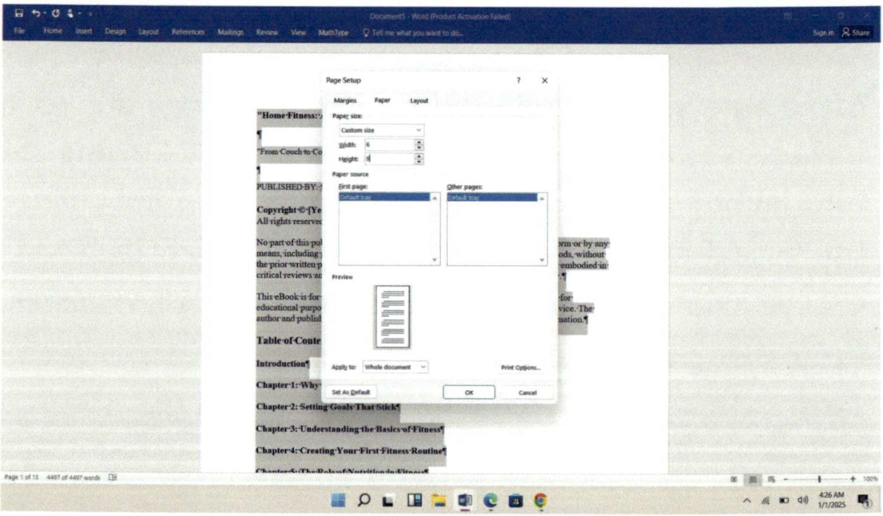

Now we will adjust the margins. Go to Layout> Click margins> click Custom margins> mirror margins> add measurements and click OK.

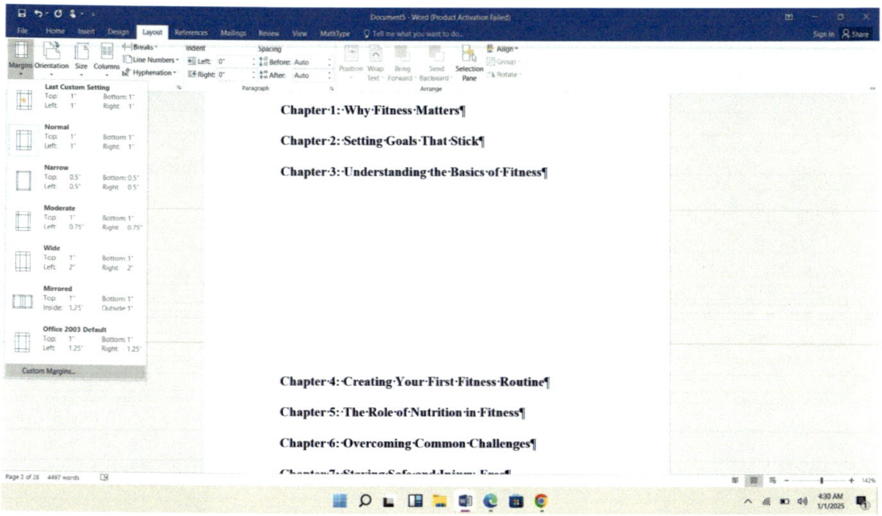

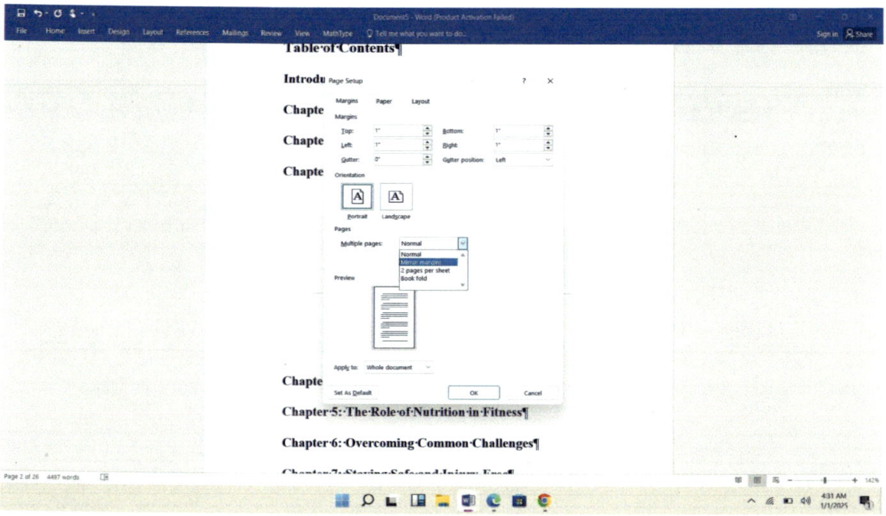

Measurement settings for mirror margins:

Top: 1

Bottom: 1

Inside: 1

Outside: 0.6

Gutter: 0.12

Gutter Position: Left

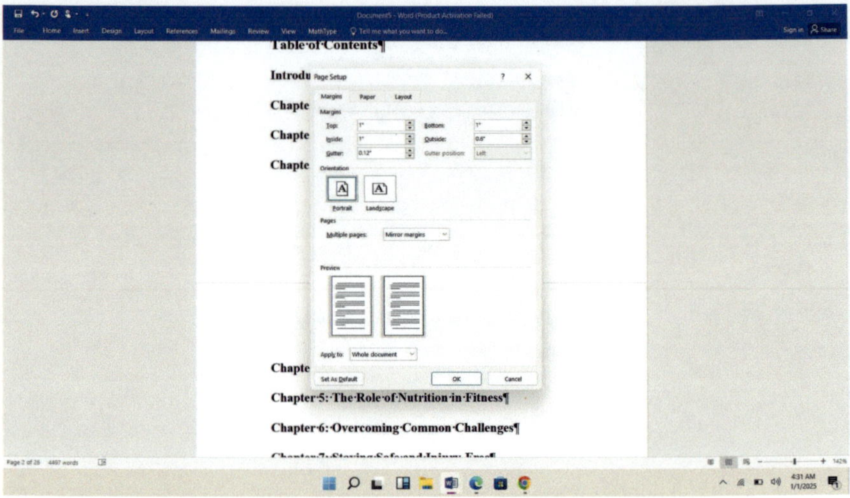

Now we will edit our content, as follows.

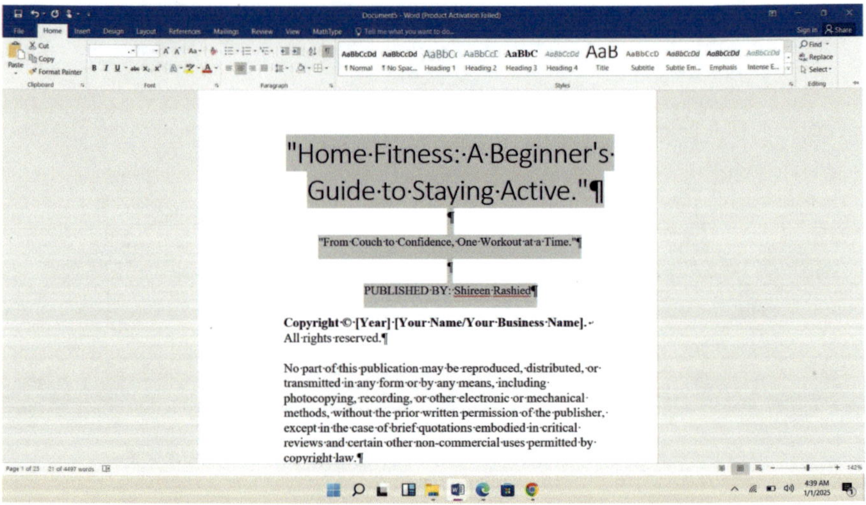

To separate the content on each page, instead of adding spaces after lines, we will add a page break at the end of our page. In this way, one page end and a new page start.

Insert > page break

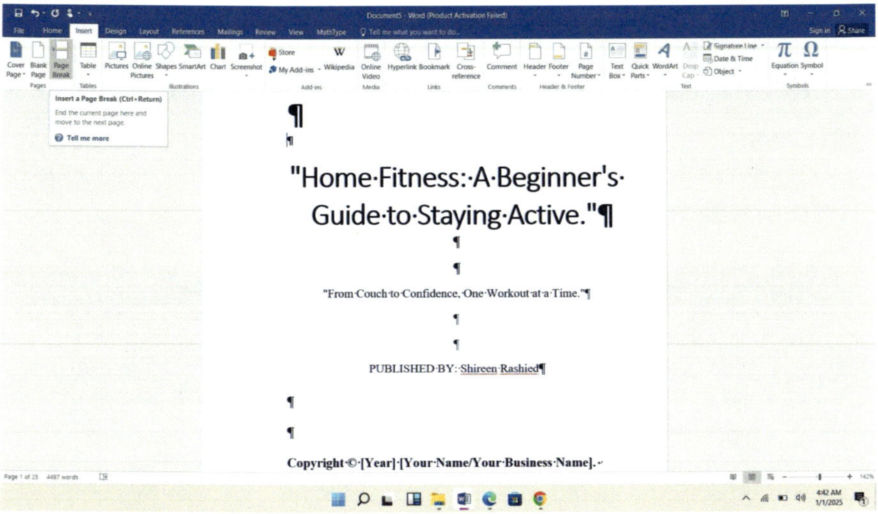

Align all the text.

Insert page break after copyright content, and follow the same process. Add page break at the end of each chapter.

Select Heading 1 for chapter heading and centre align it.

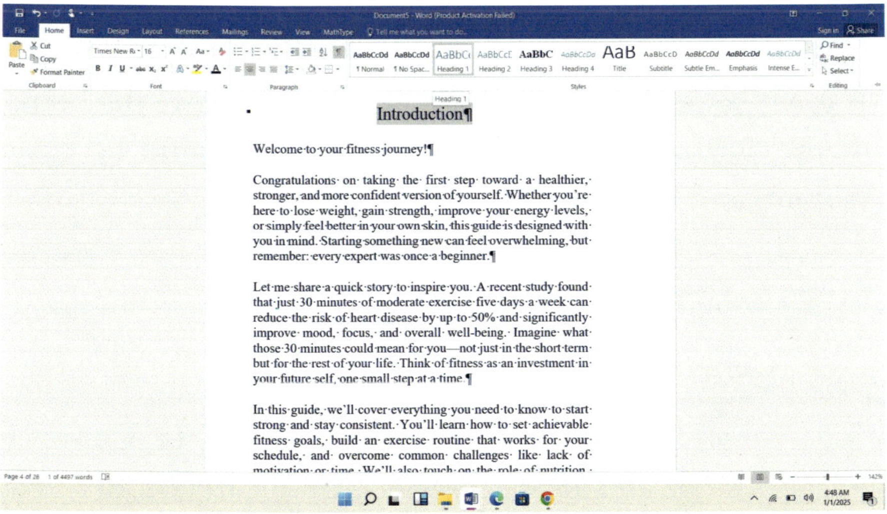

For a non-fiction book, we will add a line space.

From references, add a table of contents if you want to, as follows:

References > table of contents

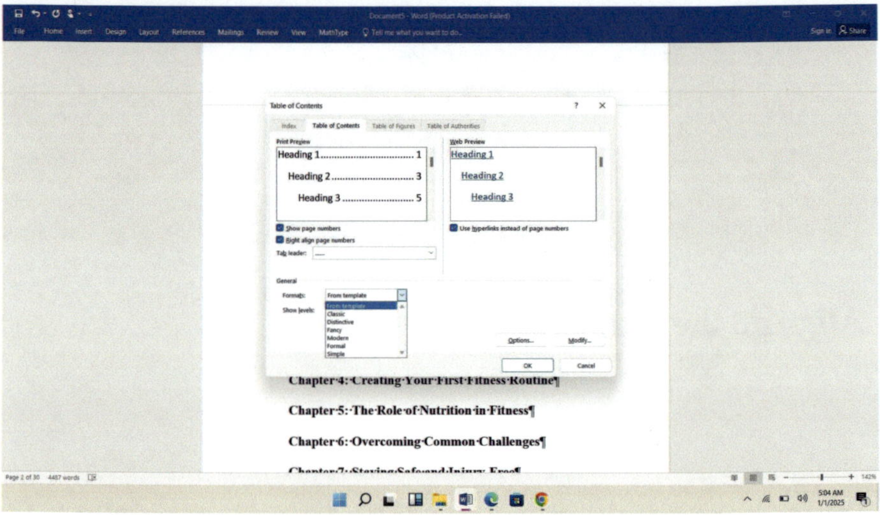

After adding the table of contents, save the document.

Save the document as PDF as well.

Designing the Book Cover

A great book cover grabs attention and conveys the book's theme. For our fitness book, the design should be clean, vibrant, and motivational.

Steps to Create the Cover:

1. **Generate Visual Ideas**:
   - Use AI tools like MidJourney or Canva to brainstorm concepts. https://canva.com

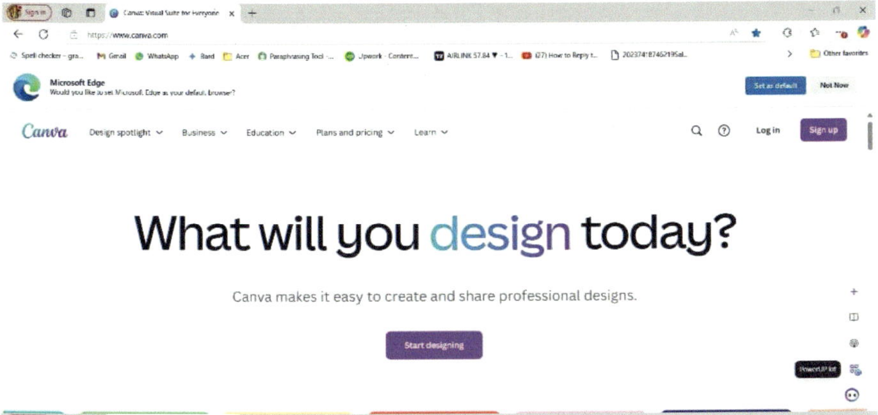

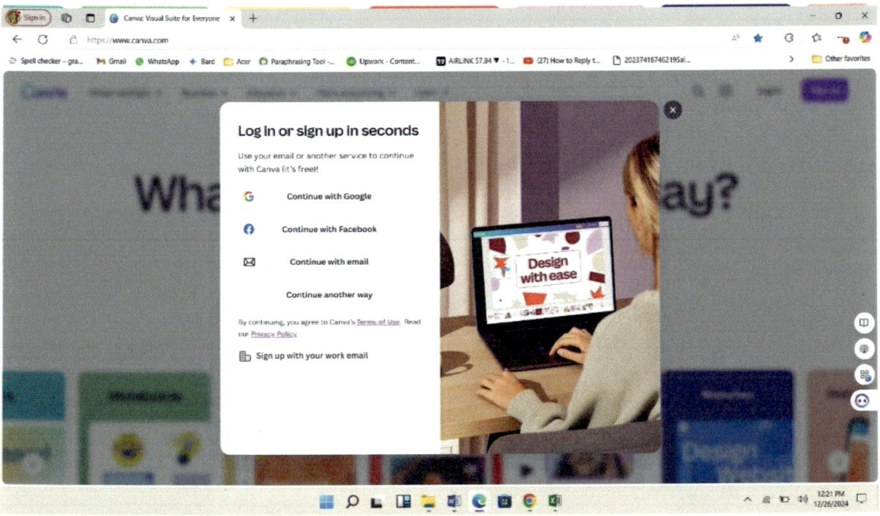

Continue with Google and choose your account.

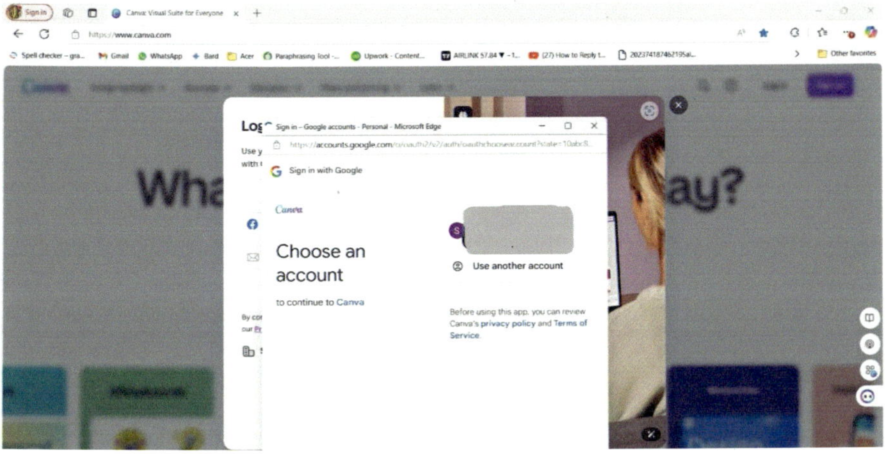

After Signing up, search for Fitness book Cover,

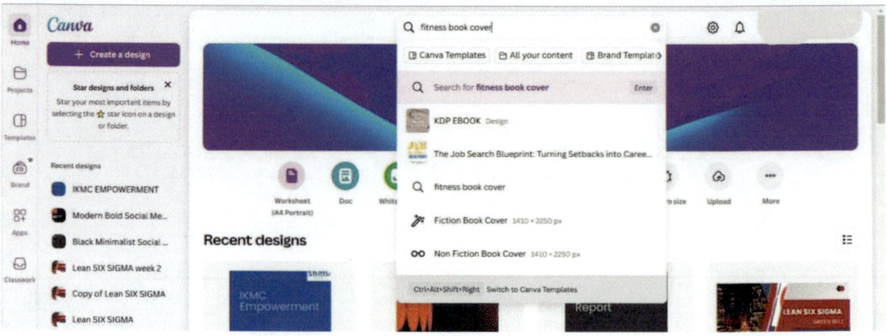

You will get a lot of designs. Scroll and select one you like.

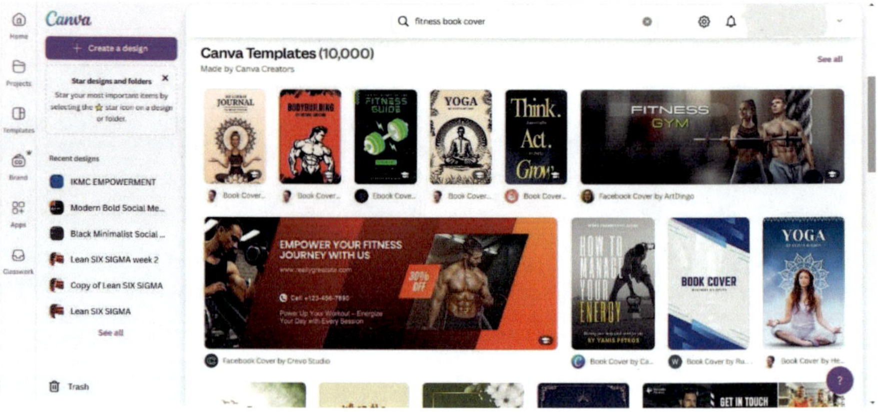

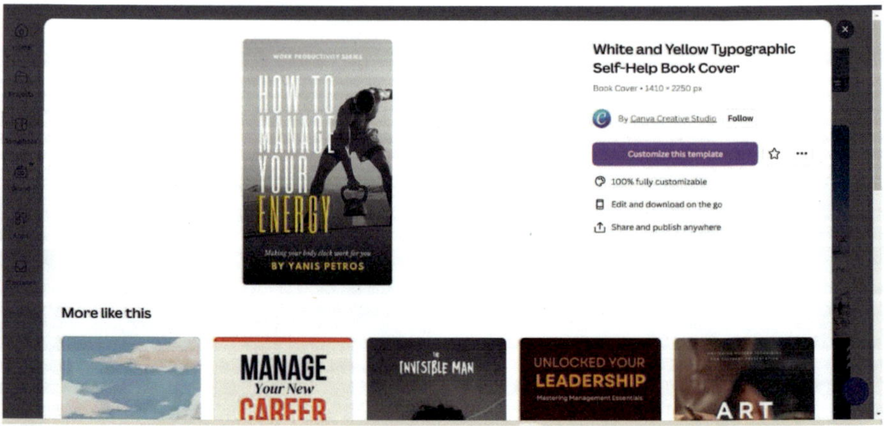

2. **Customise in Canva:**

Click customise and customise the template according to your design.

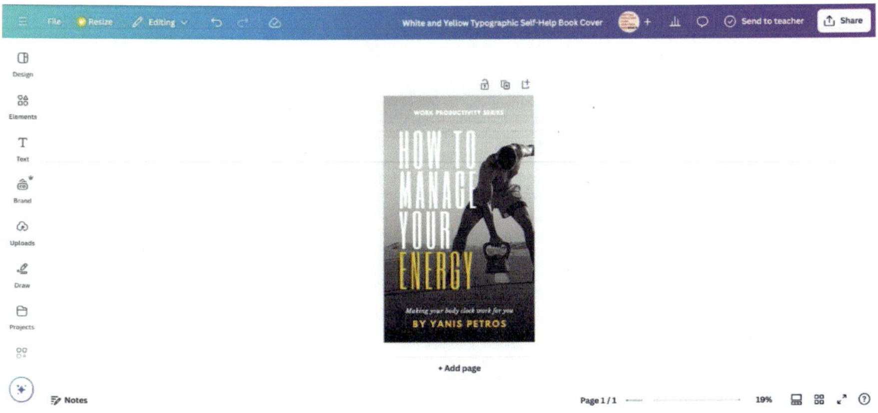

- Add the title, subtitle, and author name.
- Experiment with colours and fonts to create a professional design.

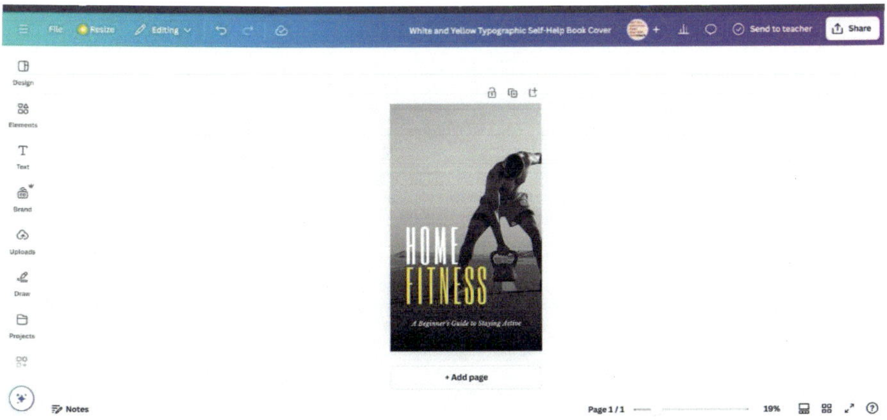

After editing click share and save the image as follows.

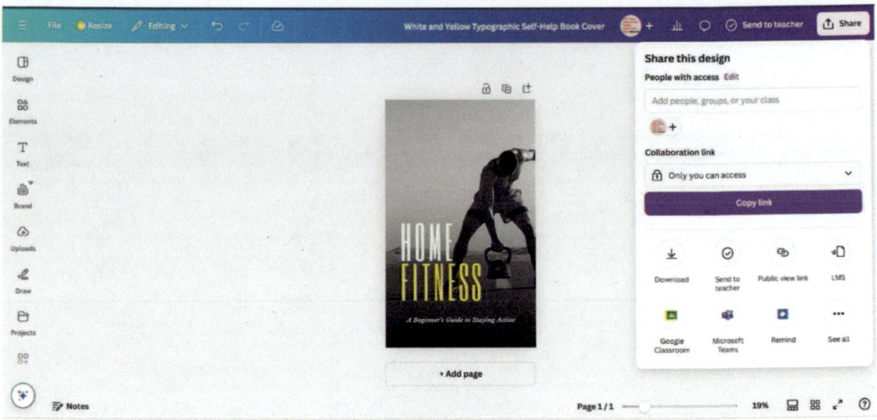

Click download and,

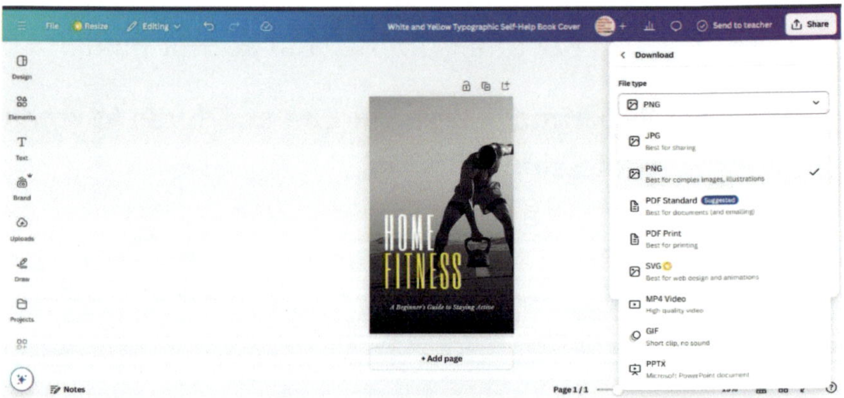

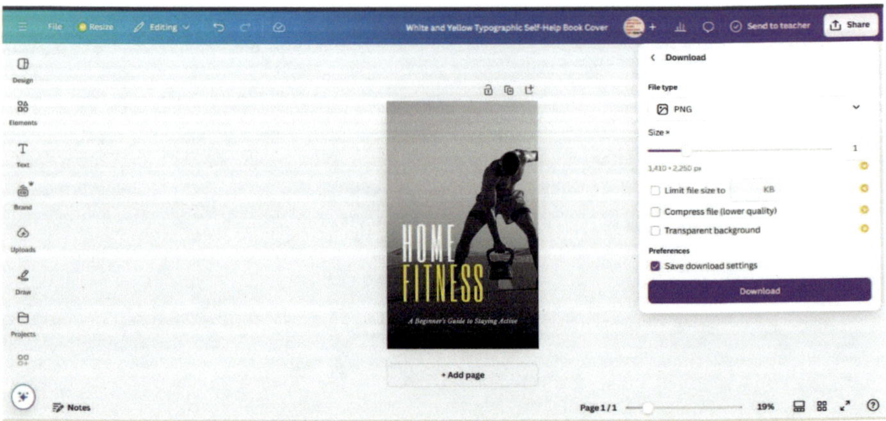

Select PNG and then click download.

3. **Ensure Correct Dimensions**:
   - For Amazon KDP, use a 6x9 inch layout for paperbacks and include space for the spine.

Now go to Google and write a KDP book cover calculator.

Binding type: paperback

Interior type: black and white

Papertype: cream paper

Reading Direction: left to right

Measurement: inches

Interior trim size: 6x9 in

Page Count: 25

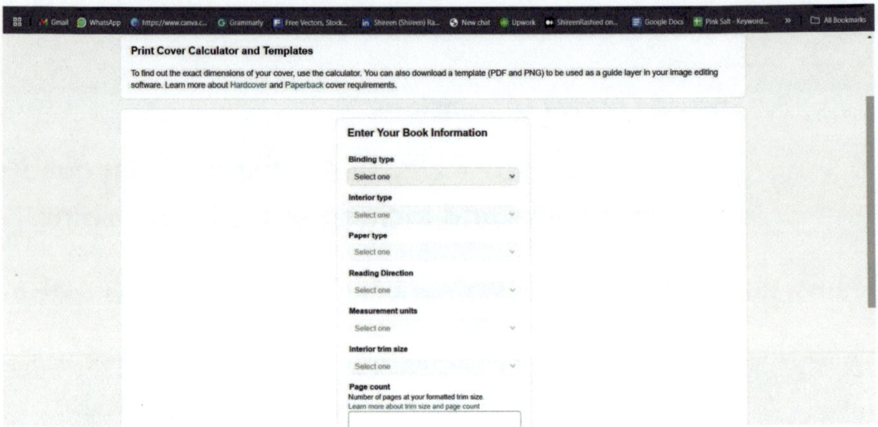

Click calculate dimensions, it will give you dimensions, press download template.

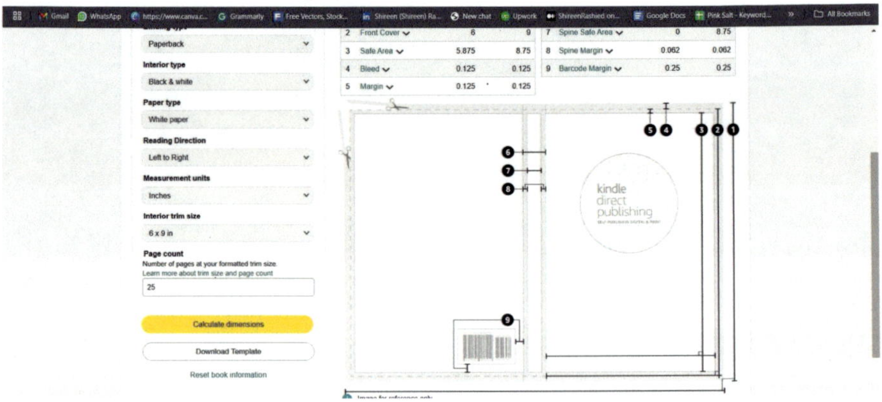

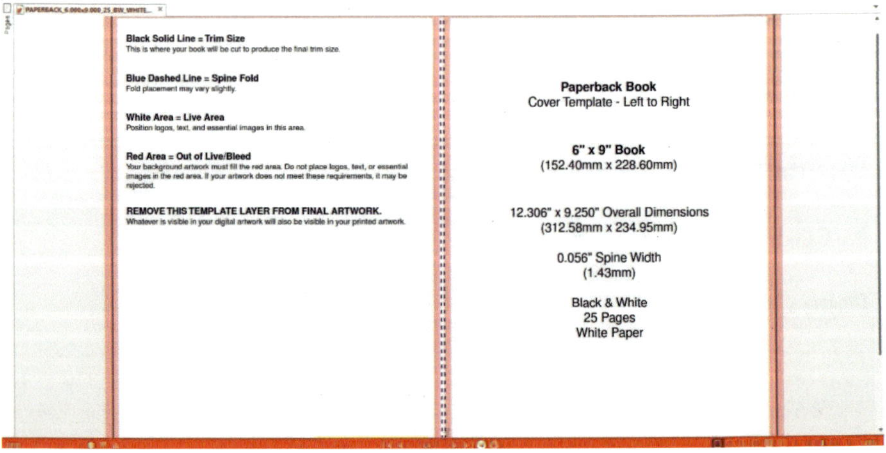

Now you have the dimensions. Format the cover as follows.

Formatting for Publishing

Before publishing, ensure the manuscript and cover meet platform requirements. For Example:

- **Manuscript:**

Go to Canva again. https://canva.com - create a design

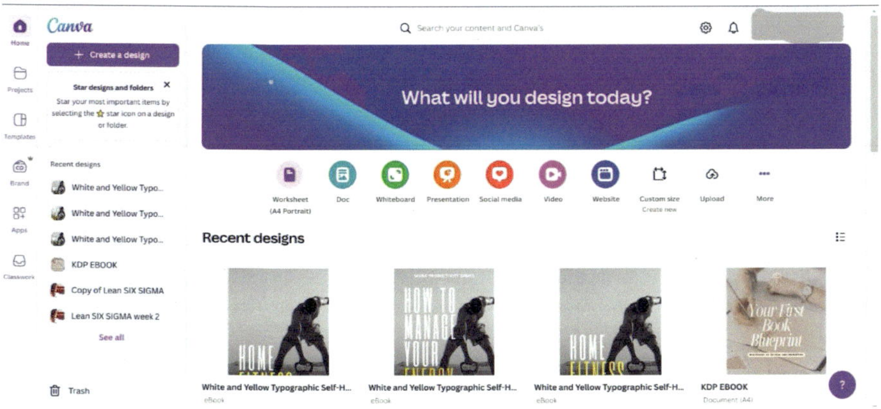

Click Custom size,

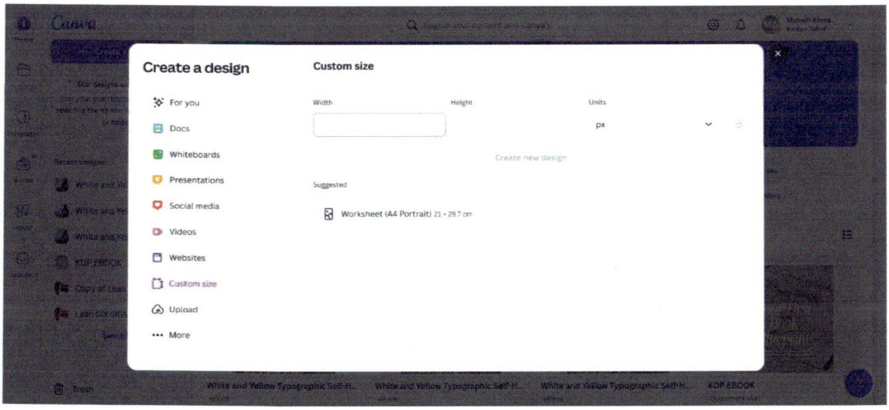

Convert px into inches and add dimensions we get from overall dimensions from the KDP book cover calculator.

12.306 x 9.25 inches

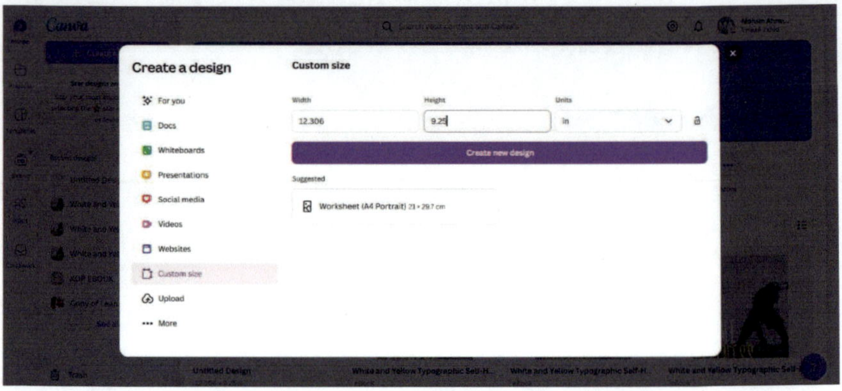

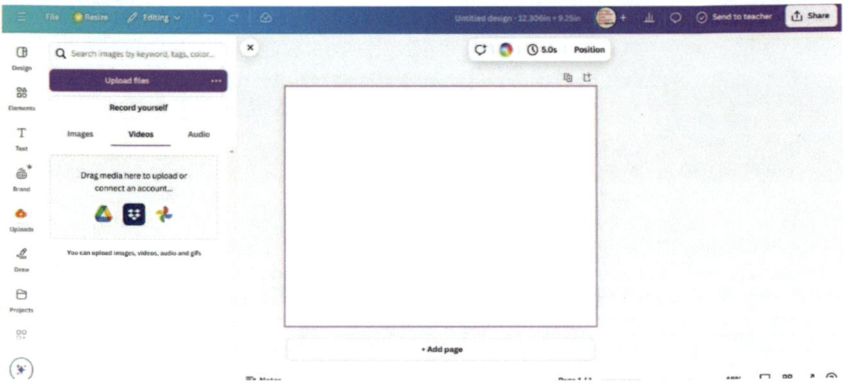

Now click upload and upload the downloaded template.

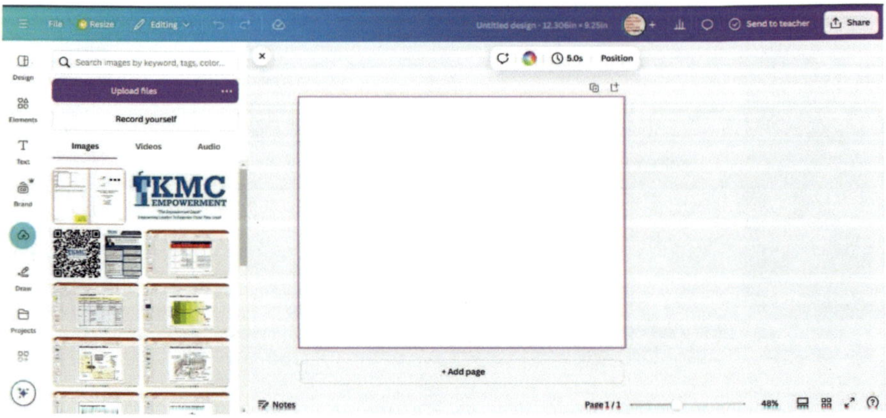

After uploading, click the template and it will be added to our custom size.

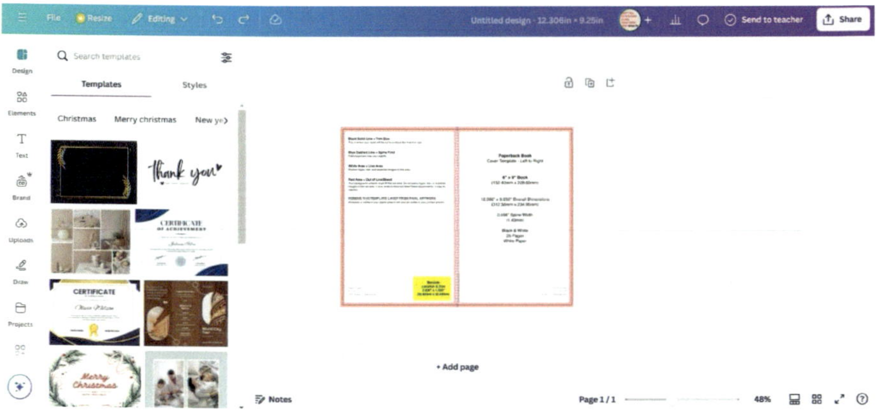

Drag it into the left corner.

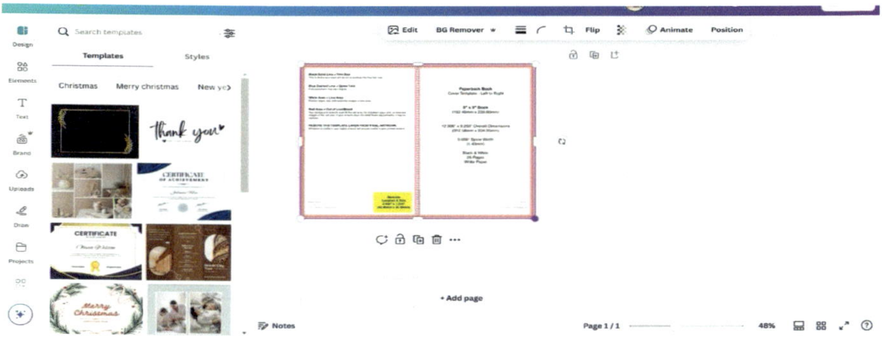

Now right click the lower right corner and drag the template over our custom size.

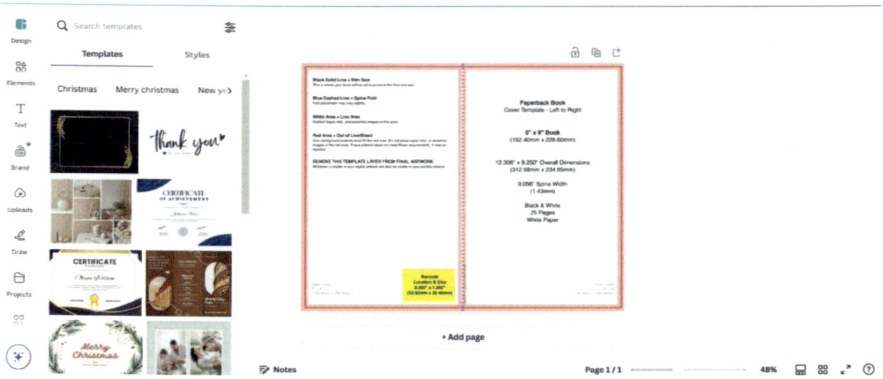

Again, go back to the uploads, and upload our cover.

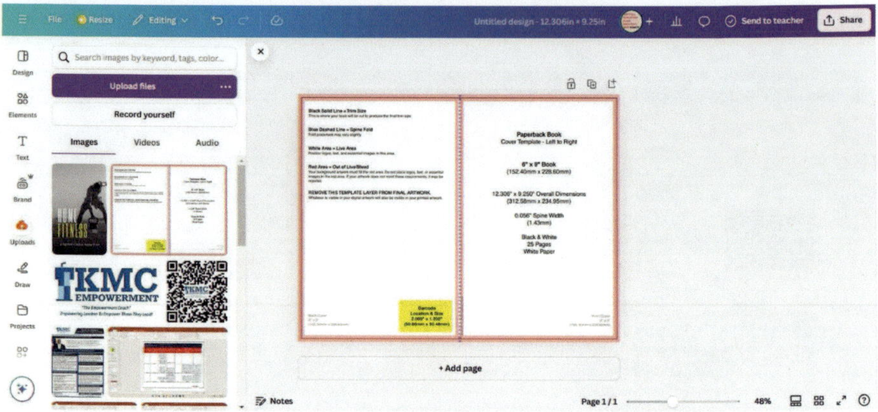

Drag the cover over the template.

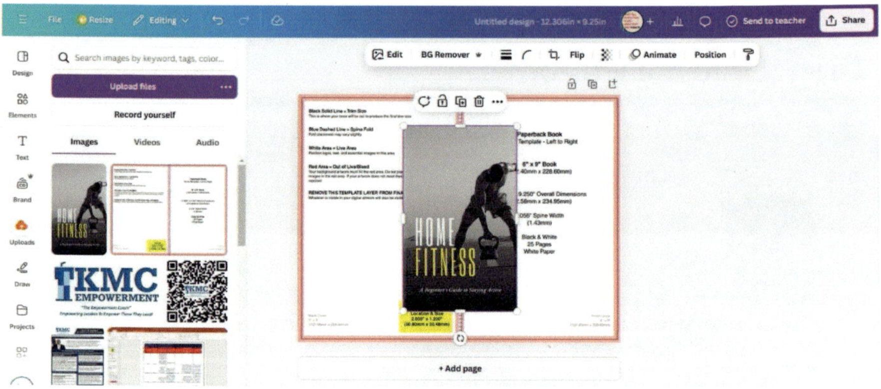

Drag the cover into the upper right corner and adjust it as follows.

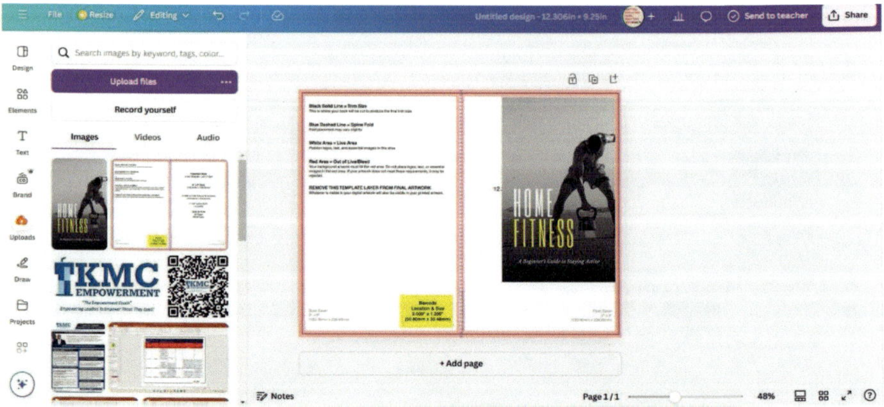

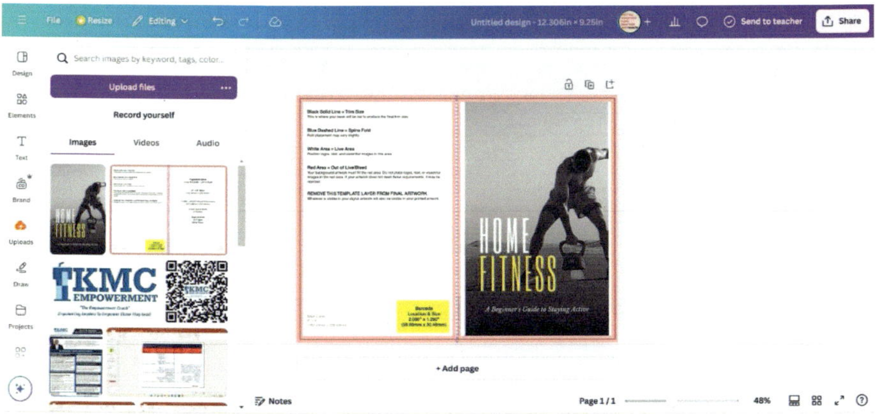

Next, go to elements and select rectangle shape and drag it to the cover template. Adjust it as follows.

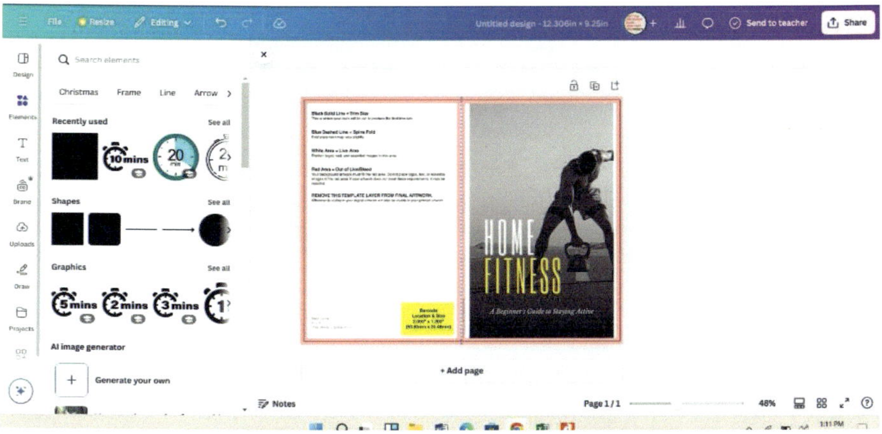

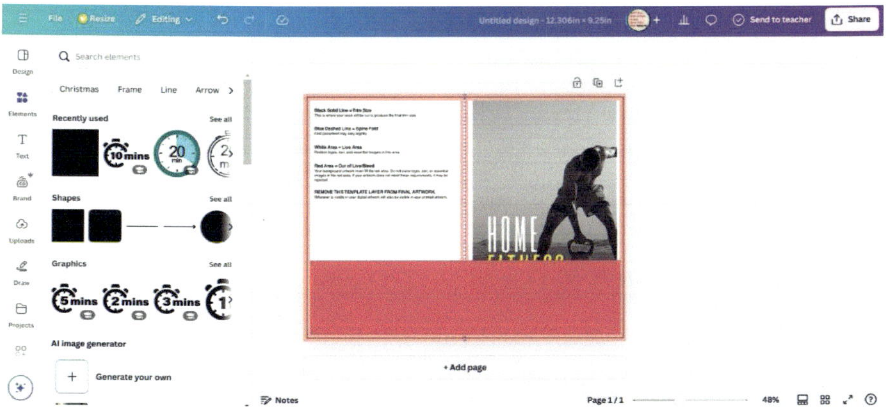

Click on rectangle and change colour as follows.

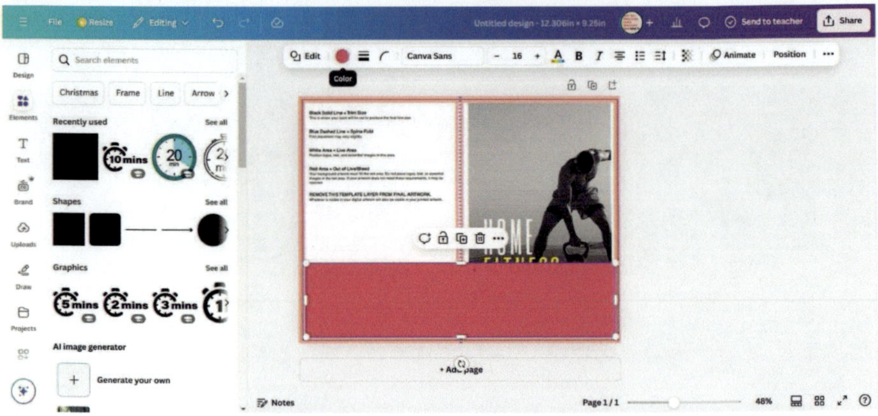

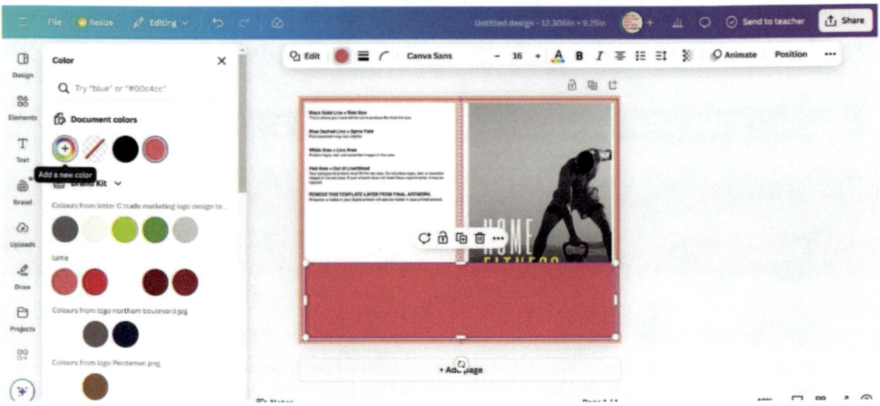

Click add new colour and then click the pen, and move it on the cover to choose your desired colour.

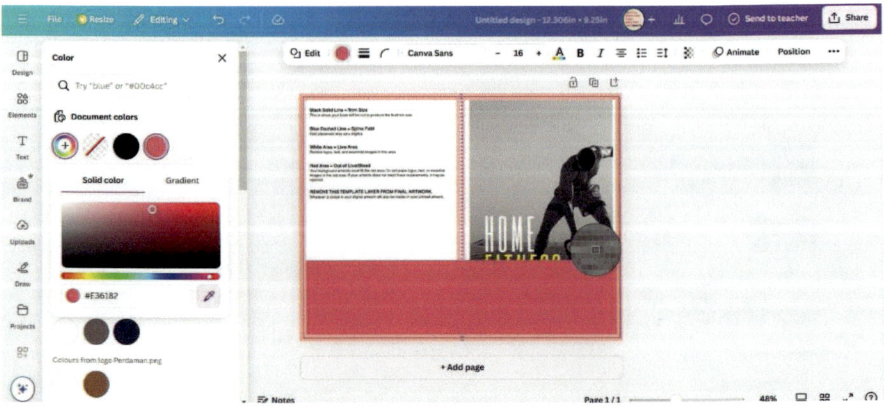

After changing the colour, expand the rectangle all over the page and position it backwords by following these steps.

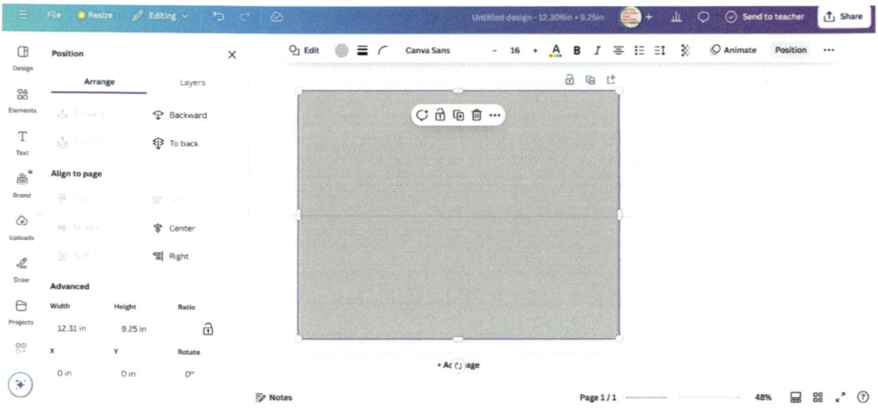

Click position > backwards

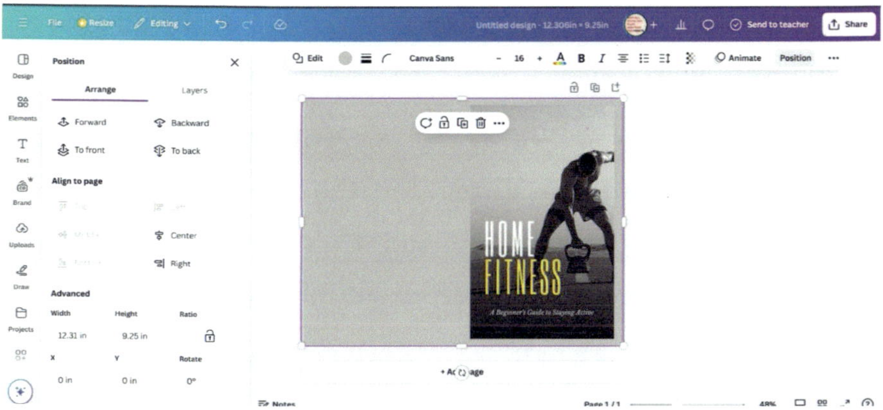

- ☐ **Go to ChatGPT and ask it to write something for the back, and place the text on the back side.**

Prompt: Write me something to put on the back of my cover.

AI Response: Back Cover Text

Start Your Fitness Journey—Right Where You Are!

No gym? No problem! Home Fitness: A Beginner's Guide to Staying Active is your perfect companion to build strength, improve health, and boost confidence—all from the comfort of your own home.

This guide is packed with:

- Beginner-friendly exercises you can do anywhere.
- Practical tips for setting and achieving your fitness goals.
- Easy-to-follow routines that fit your schedule.
- Nutrition and hydration advice to fuel your progress.
- Motivational strategies to keep you moving, even on tough days.

Whether you're a complete beginner or getting back into fitness, this book gives you the tools, guidance, and inspiration to make fitness a part of your lifestyle—no expensive equipment or gym memberships required.

Your journey to a healthier, happier you starts here. Let's take that first step together!

Ready to transform your life? Open the book and let's get moving!

- Format to 6x9 inches with proper margins on the download section.

Cover:

- Export as a high-resolution PDF or PNG.

- Download the cover as JPG.

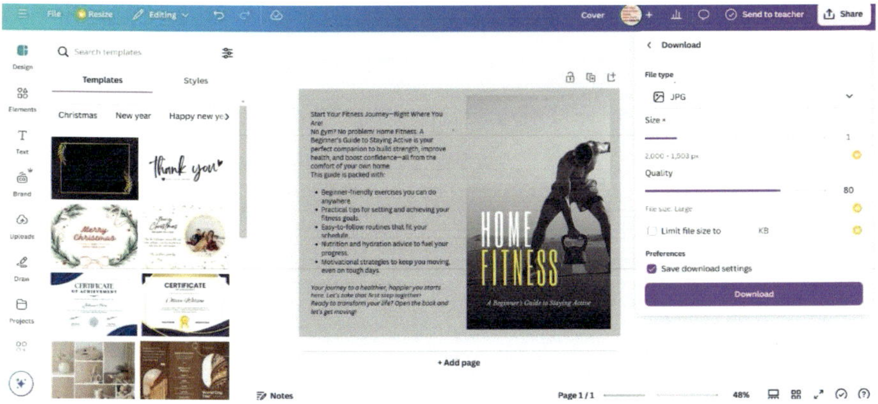

Use Amazon's cover calculator to adjust spine dimensions based on page count.

Exercise: Create Your Fitness Book

Follow these steps to create your fitness guide:

1. Use AI to brainstorm and complete a title.
2. Develop a chapter outline with clear goals and subtopics.
3. Draft an introduction that inspires and engages readers.
4. Write one chapter in detail, using AI to assist with examples and instructions.
5. Design a cover that reflects the theme and message of your book.

By completing these steps, you'll have a well-rounded book ready for further refinement and publishing.

Conclusion

Creating a fitness book is a rewarding experience that combines creativity, knowledge, and AI-powered tools. You now have a step-by-step example to follow, showing how to turn an idea into a fully formed manuscript. In the next module, you'll learn how to publish this book on Amazon KDP and make it available to readers worldwide. Get ready to take the next step in your author journey!

Module 4

Publishing Your Book on Amazon KDP

Now that your manuscript is ready, it's time to take the exciting step of publishing your book. Amazon Kindle Direct Publishing (KDP) provides an accessible platform to share your work with a global audience. This guide will walk you through the entire process, ensuring you know exactly how to prepare, upload, and publish your book effectively.

Why Publish with Amazon KDP?

Amazon KDP offers unparalleled opportunities for authors. Here's why it's an ideal choice for self-publishing:

- **Global Reach**: Your book is available to millions of readers worldwide.
- **Royalties**: Earn up to 70% royalties on ebook sales and keep significant profits for paperbacks.
- **Ease of Use**: User-friendly tools and step-by-step guidance make it accessible to authors of all experience levels.

- **Print-on-Demand**: No upfront costs or inventory requirements; Amazon prints your book when readers order it.
- **Multiple Formats**: Publish ebooks, paperbacks, and even hardcovers.

Setting Up Your Amazon KDP Account

Before you can publish your book, you need an Amazon KDP account. Here are the steps to set it up:

1. **Visit the KDP Website**:
    - Go to kdp.amazon.com.

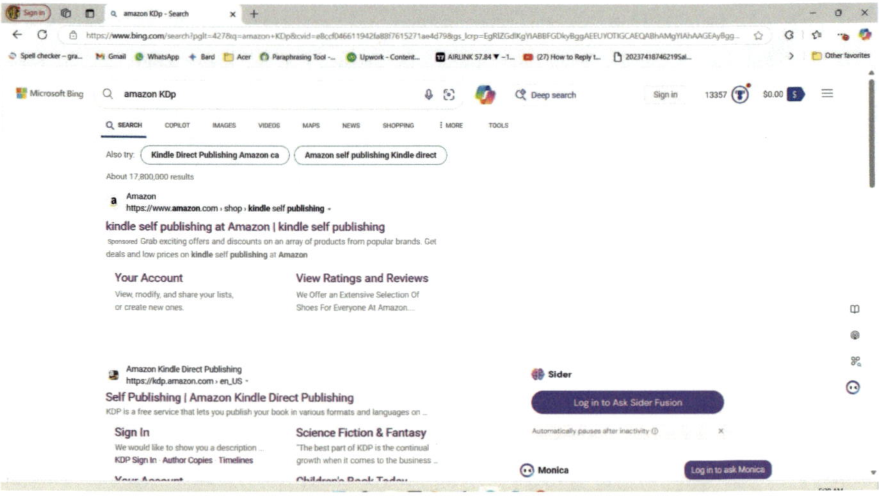

2. **Sign In or Create an Amazon Account**:
    - If you already have an Amazon account, sign in using your existing credentials.
    - If you don't have an account, click "Create your KDP account" and fill in the required details, including your email address and password.

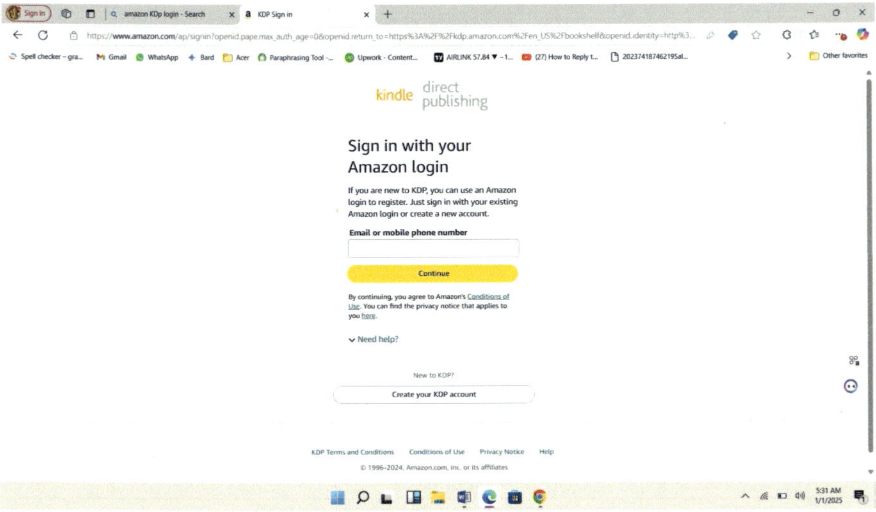

Click Create your KDP account and enter the required information.

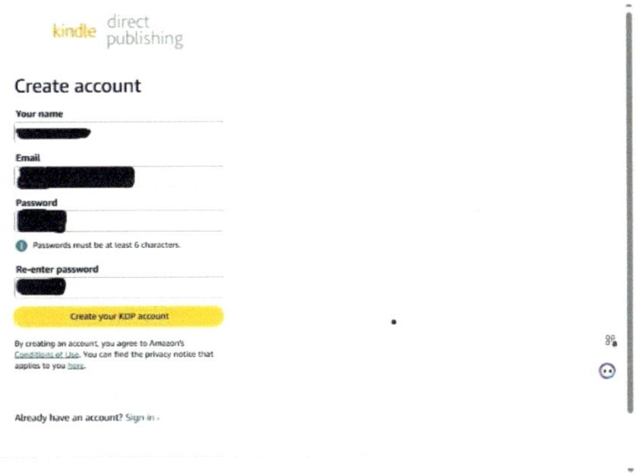

3. **Complete Your Account Information**:

   - Once logged in, go to the "Your Account" section.
   - Fill out the details:
     - **Author/Publisher Name:** This will appear in your payments and reports.

- **Tax Information**: Provide your tax ID or Social Security Number (SSN) to comply with IRS regulations.
- **Bank Details:** Enter your bank account information to receive royalty payments. Ensure you use accurate details to avoid delays.

4. **Set Your Payment Preferences**:
    - Choose your preferred currency and payment method. Direct deposit is the most convenient option for timely payments.
5. **Review and Save**:
    - Double-check your information and click "Save."

Your KDP account is now ready, and you can create and publish your book.

KDP Formatting and Cover Dimensions

Proper formatting and cover design are critical to ensure your book meets Amazon's standards and looks professional.

Manuscript Formatting Guidelines

1. **Page Dimensions**:
    - For print books, standard sizes include:
        - 6 x 9 inches (most popular for paperbacks).
        - 5.5 x 8.5 inches (great for smaller books).

- 8.5 x 11 inches (ideal for workbooks or children's books).

2. **Margins**:
    - Maintain at least 0.25 inches of margin on all sides for print.
    - For books with over 150 pages, increase the gutter margin (inner margin) to accommodate binding.
3. **Font and Layout**:
    - Use readable fonts like Times New Roman, Arial, or Garamond, with a size of 11 or 12 points.
    - Align text to the left; avoid fully justified text to prevent awkward spacing.
    - Use consistent spacing and headers for a polished look.
4. **File Format**:
    - Upload your manuscript in .docx for ebooks.
    - Save your manuscript as a high-quality PDF for print.
5. **Check for Errors**:
    - Use Amazon's preview tool to ensure formatting appears as intended on different devices or print previews.

Cover Dimensions and Design Guidelines

1. **Cover Dimensions**:
   - Covers must include a front, back, and spine (for print books).
   - Use Amazon's cover calculator to determine exact dimensions based on page count.
   - For a 6 x 9-inch book with 100 pages, the recommended cover dimensions (with bleed) are:
     - **Front Cover:** 6.125 x 9.25 inches
     - **Back Cover:** 6.125 x 9.25 inches
     - **Spine Width:** 0.23 inches
2. **Resolution**:
   - Ensure your cover is high resolution (at least 300 DPI) to avoid pixilation.
3. **File Format**:
   - Save your cover as a high-quality PDF or PNG.
4. **Colour Mode**:
   - Use CMYK colour mode for print covers.
   - Use RGB colour mode for ebook covers.
5. **Avoid Critical Content in Bleed Areas**:
   - Ensure no text or important visuals are in the bleed area (edges that may be trimmed during printing).

6. **Cover Content**:
   - Include the title, subtitle, and author name on the front cover.
   - Optionally, include a tagline or testimonial for added appeal.
   - The back cover can feature a summary, author bio, and barcode.

7. **Design Tools**:
   - Use Amazon's Cover Creator or external tools like Canva and Adobe Photoshop for professional results.

Preparing to Publish

Before uploading your book to KDP, ensure everything is formatted and ready for submission. A polished manuscript and professional cover are essential to make a strong first impression.

Finalizing the Manuscript

- Format your manuscript to the correct size. For paperbacks, 6x9 inches is a common choice.
- Use consistent fonts and spacing. Ensure chapter titles are styled uniformly.
- Convert your manuscript into the required formats:
  - Save as a .docx file for Kindle ebooks.
  - Save as a high-quality PDF for print.

Polishing the Cover Design

- Make sure your cover dimensions align with KDP's requirements. Use Amazon's cover calculator to determine spine width based on your page count.
- Save your cover file as a high-resolution PDF or PNG.

Creating a New Book on KDP

Once your materials are ready, log in to your KDP account and follow these steps to create your book listing.

Step 1: Starting a New Project

Once you have created your account and enter the account details, you will be ready to upload your first book. You will be directed to the following page.

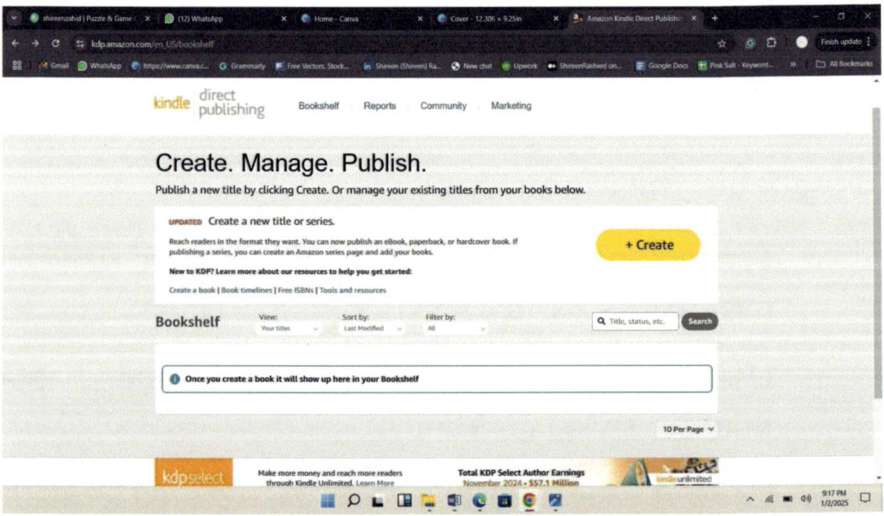

- Navigate to your KDP dashboard and select "Create a New Title."

- Choose whether you're publishing a Kindle ebook, paperback, or hardcover.

After clicking the page, you will be directed to the next page. Click on CREATE EBOOK.

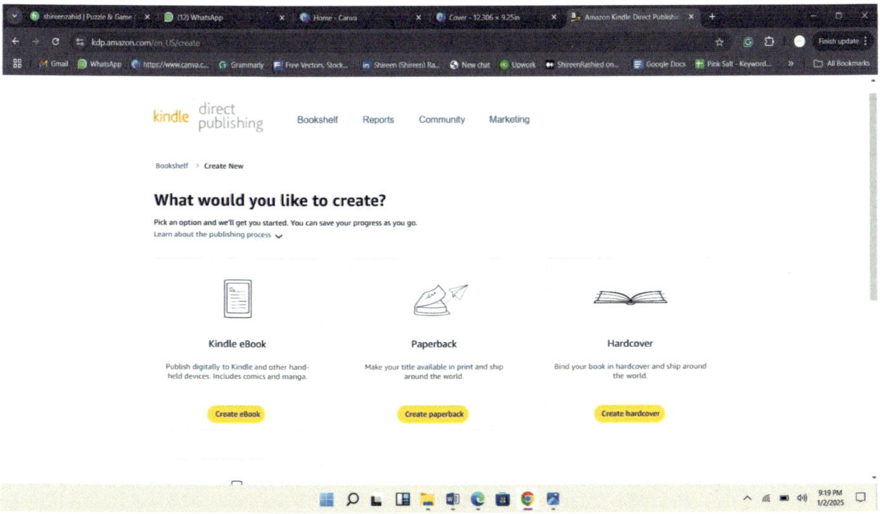

You will be directed to enter book details in the next step.

Step 2: Entering Book Details

- Select your language, I have entered English.
- Add your book title and subtitle. These should clearly communicate the book's purpose.
- If you are going to create a series, then add it, otherwise ignore the series and Edition Number.
- Input the author's name and contributors, if applicable.
- Write a compelling book description. This section will help sell your book to potential readers.

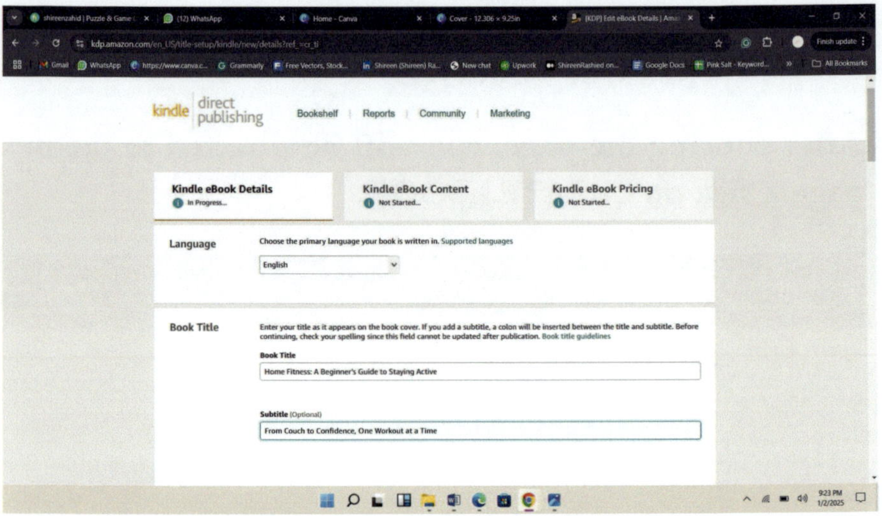

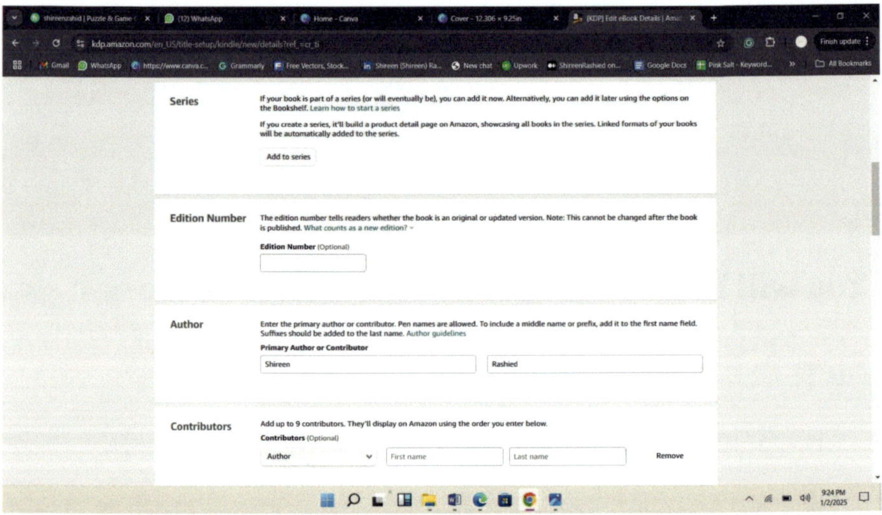

Example Prompt for Description: I want an Amazon product description of my book with a call to action at the end.

AI Response: Transform Your Home into a Fitness Haven—No Gym Required!

Are you ready to take control of your fitness but unsure where to start? Home Fitness: A Beginner's Guide to Staying

Active is the ultimate guide to building healthy habits, improving your strength, and boosting your energy—all from the comfort of your own home.

This easy-to-follow book is designed for beginners, offering practical advice, step-by-step routines, and motivational tips to help you kick start your fitness journey. Whether you're looking to lose weight, tone up, or simply feel better in your daily life, this guide has everything you need to get started.

Inside, You'll Discover:

- The benefits of fitness for your body, mind, and lifestyle.
- Beginner-friendly exercises you can do anywhere—no fancy equipment needed!
- How to set realistic fitness goals using the SMART framework.
- A complete guide to building your first fitness routine, tailored to your schedule.
- The role of balanced nutrition and hydration in maximising your results.
- Tips for staying consistent, overcoming challenges, and avoiding injuries.
- How to track your progress and celebrate your wins, big or small.

With simple explanations, actionable steps, and plenty of encouragement, this guide takes the guesswork out of starting your fitness journey. It's not about perfection—it's about progress, and this book is here to guide you every step of the way.

Don't wait to transform your health and happiness. Take the first step toward an active lifestyle today!

Ready to Get Started?

Click "Buy Now" and begin your journey to a healthier, stronger, and more confident YOU—all from the comfort of home!

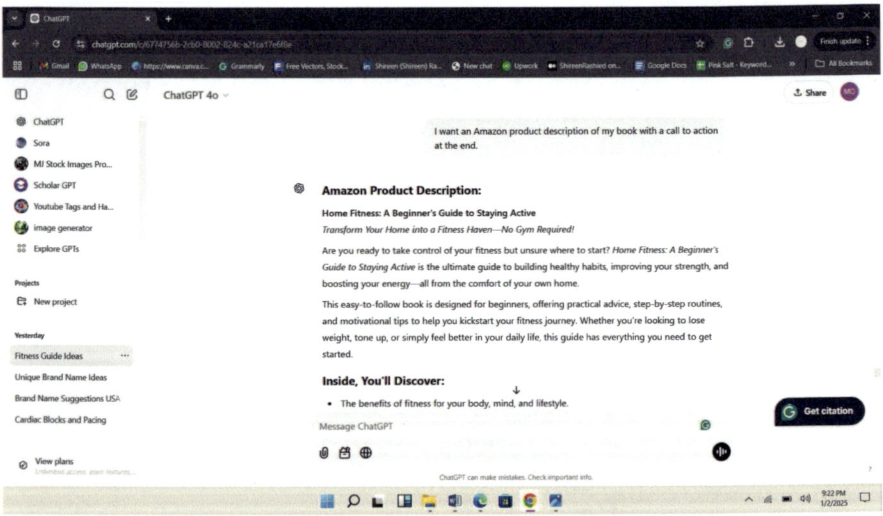

After adding a description, click the right options.

Click: I own the publishing rights.

Click **Yes** if you have sexual images, or **No** if you don't have any.

Step 3: Choosing Keywords and Categories

- Pick two categories that align with your book's content, such as "Health, Fitness and Dieting" or "Exercise & Fitness."

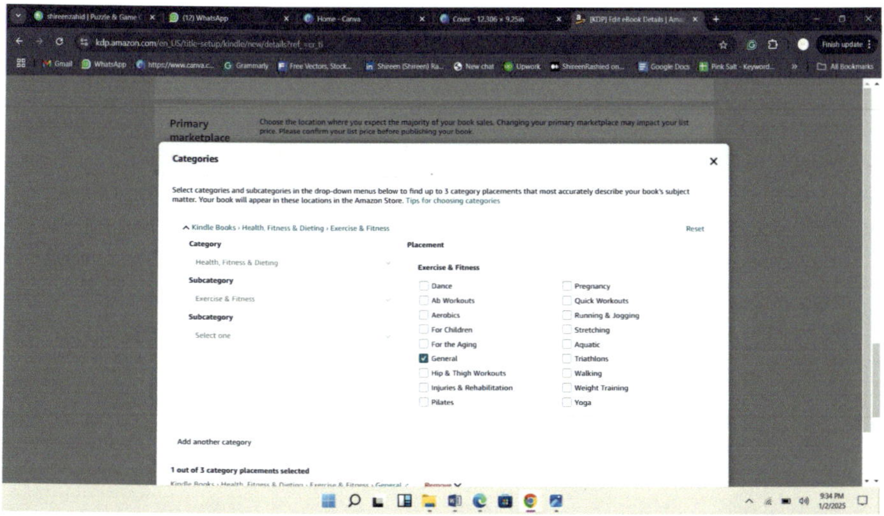

- Click Save.

- Select up to seven keywords that help readers find your book. Think about terms your audience might search for.

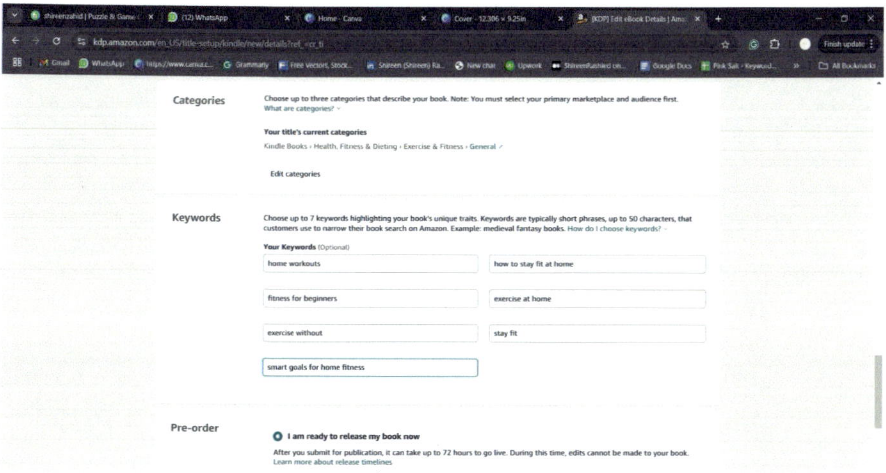

- Example: "home workouts," "fitness for beginners," "exercise without equipment."

- Save and Continue.

Uploading Your Files

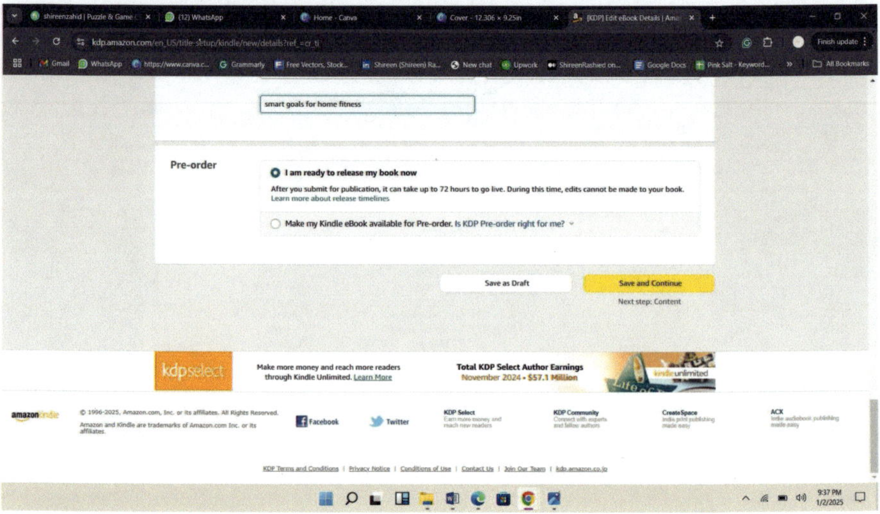

Manuscript Upload

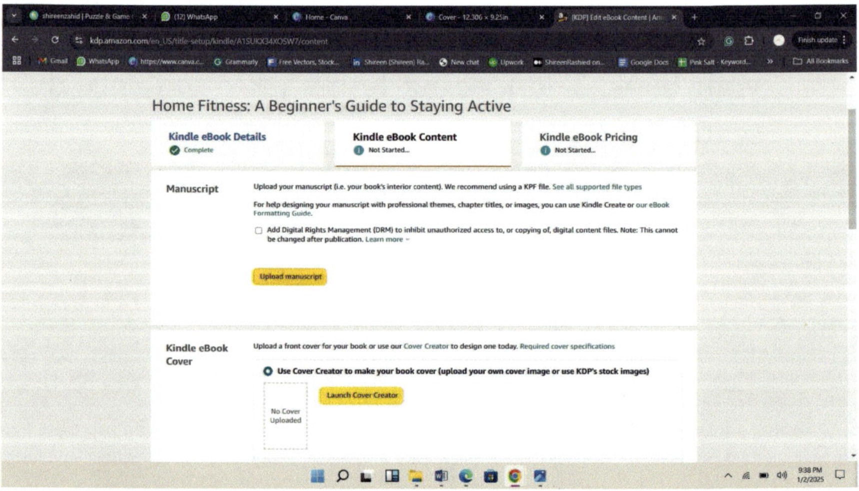

- Upload your formatted manuscript. For Kindle ebooks, use .docx; for paperbacks, upload a PDF.

- Use KDP's preview tool to review how your book will appear on various devices or in print. Ensure there are no formatting errors.

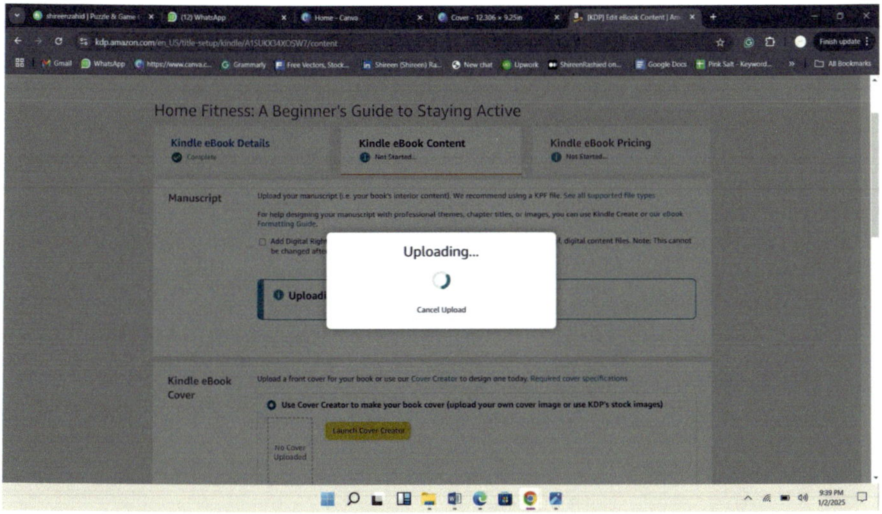

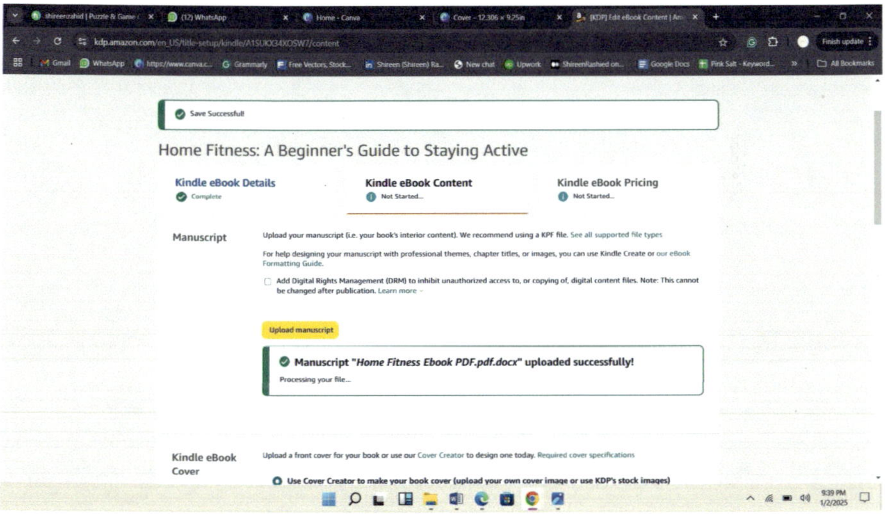

Cover Upload

- Upload your cover file. Make sure it matches the specified dimensions and includes bleed.

- Preview the cover to verify that the design aligns properly, especially around the spine.
- Click upload cover you already have.
- Upload the cover you have created through Canva.

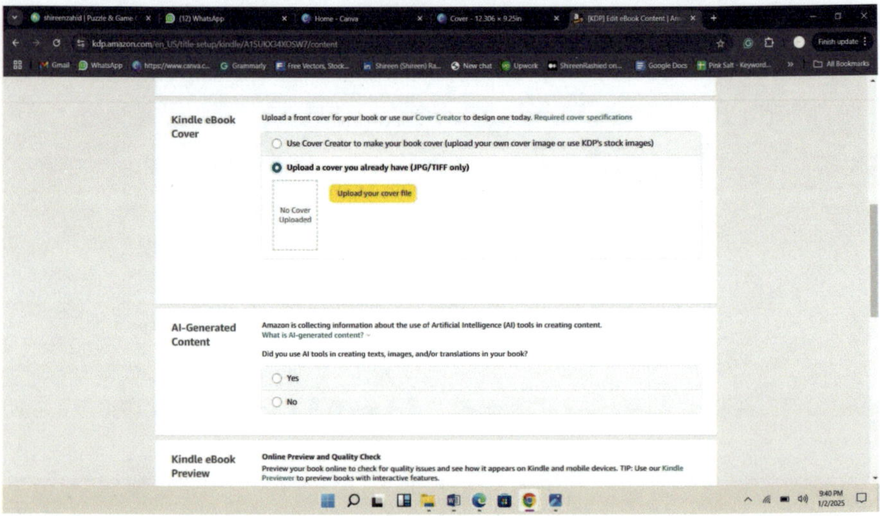

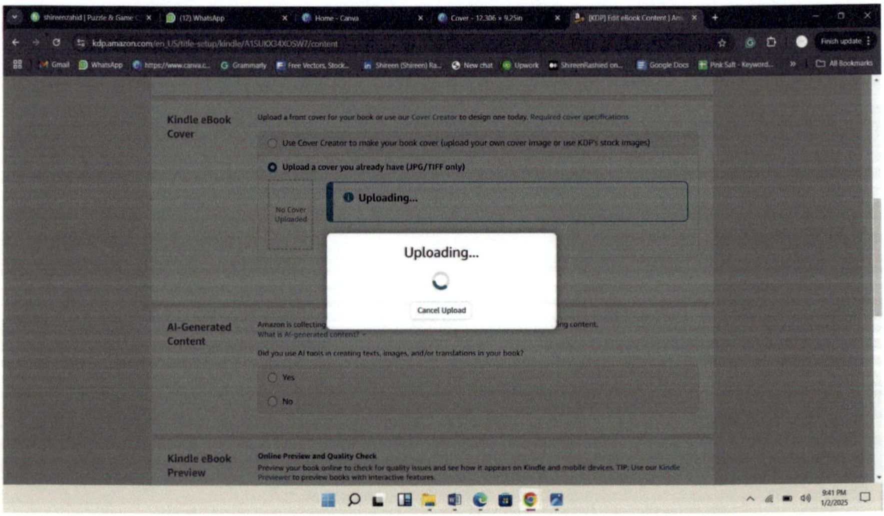

- Next, fill out the following details.

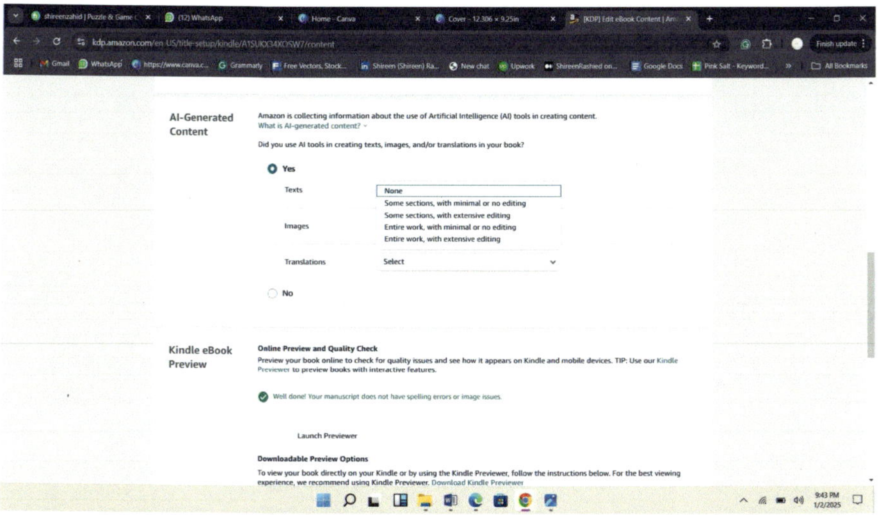

- Then click **Launch Previewer** to check your Ebook.

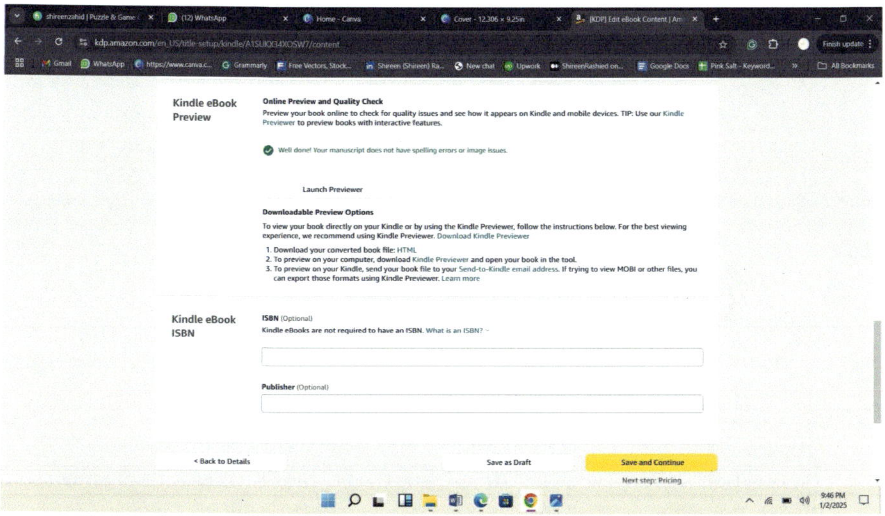

- It will take a few seconds.

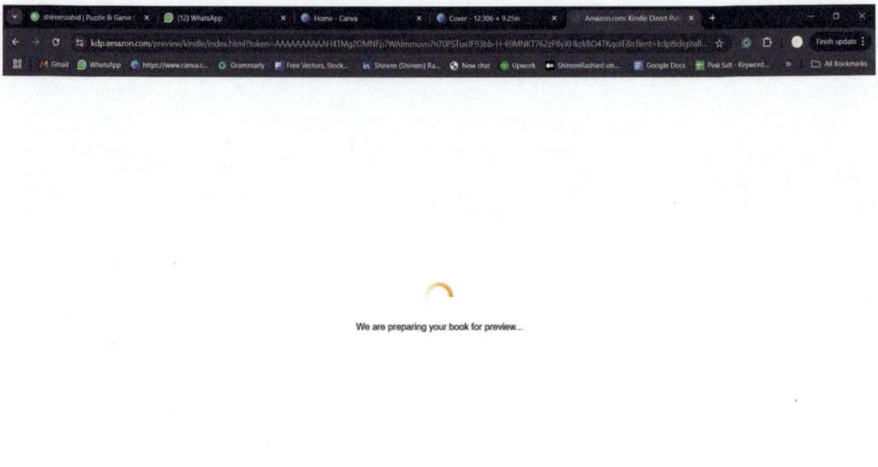
We are preparing your book for preview...

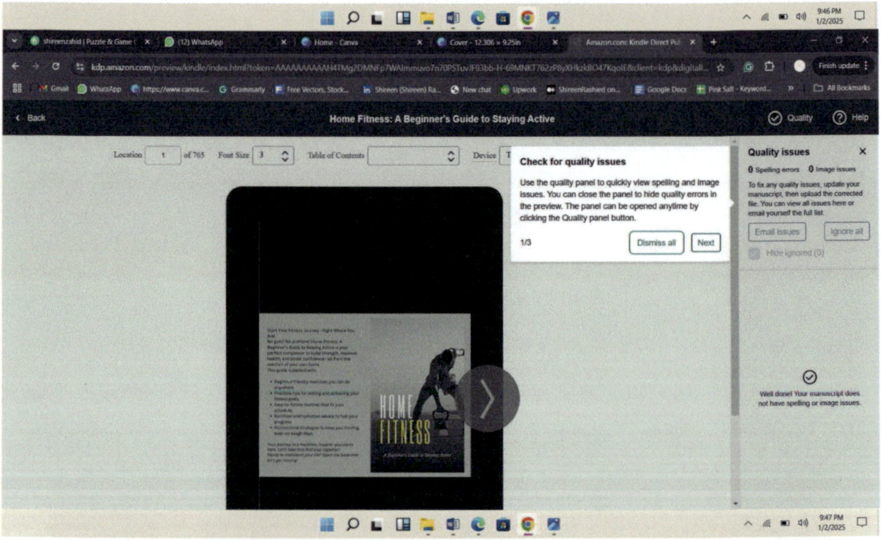
Back
Home Fitness: A Beginner's Guide to Staying Active
Quality
Help
Location
of 765
Font Size
Table of Contents
Device
Check for quality issues
Use the quality panel to quickly view spelling and image issues. You can close the panel to hide quality errors in the preview. The panel can be opened anytime by clicking the Quality panel button.
1/3
Dismiss all
Next
Quality issues
0 Spelling errors 0 Image issues
To fix any quality issues, update your manuscript, then upload the corrected file. You can view all issues here or email yourself the full list.
Email issues
Ignore all
Hide ignored (0)
Well done! Your manuscript does not have spelling or image issues.
HOME
FITNESS

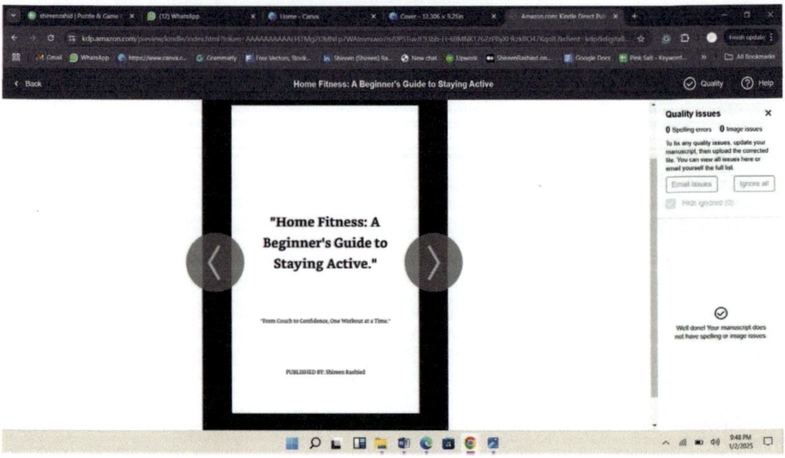
Back
Home Fitness: A Beginner's Guide to Staying Active
Quality
Help
"Home Fitness: A Beginner's Guide to Staying Active."
"From Couch to Confidence, One Workout at a Time."
PUBLISHED BY: Shireen Rashied
Quality issues
0 Spelling errors 0 Image issues
Well done! Your manuscript does not have spelling or image issues.

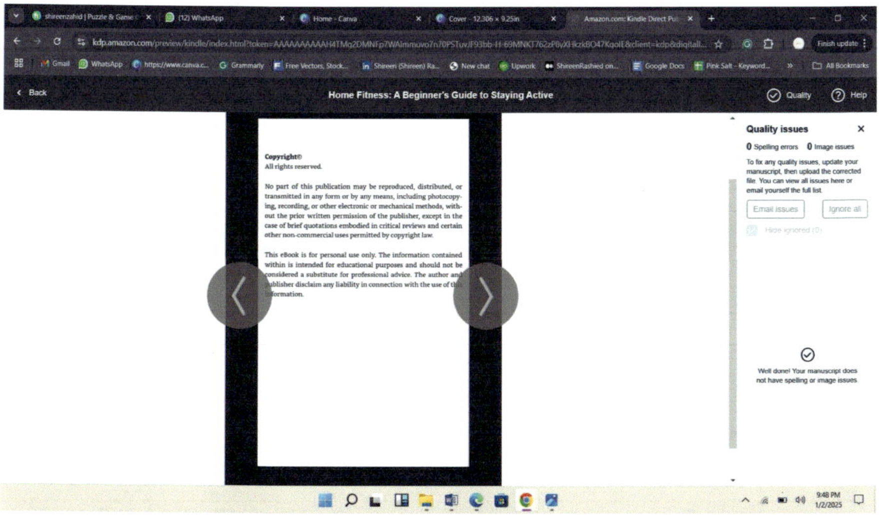

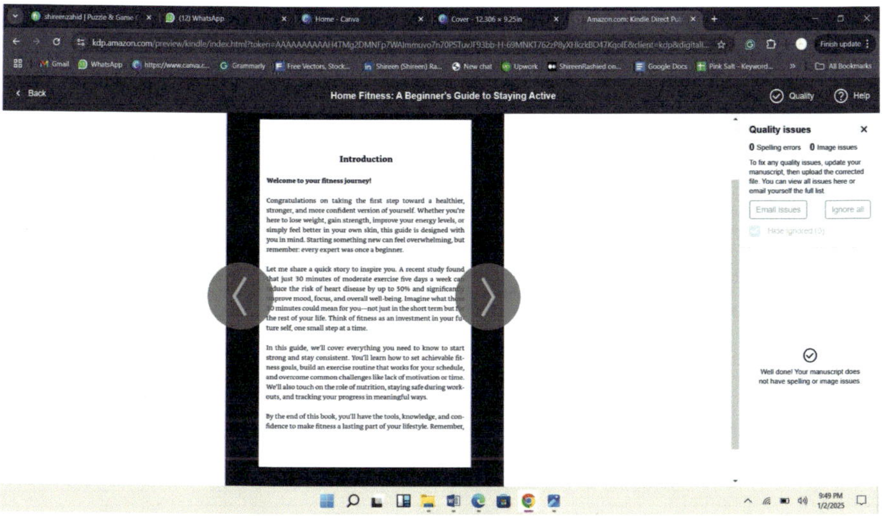

- Check the preview carefully.
- You don't have to add any ISBN, as Amazon KDP will provide you with this.
- Click Save and Continue.

Setting Pricing and Royalties

Deciding on your book's price is a critical step. KDP allows you to set prices for both ebooks and paperbacks, giving you control over your earnings.

- You will be directed to the next page.

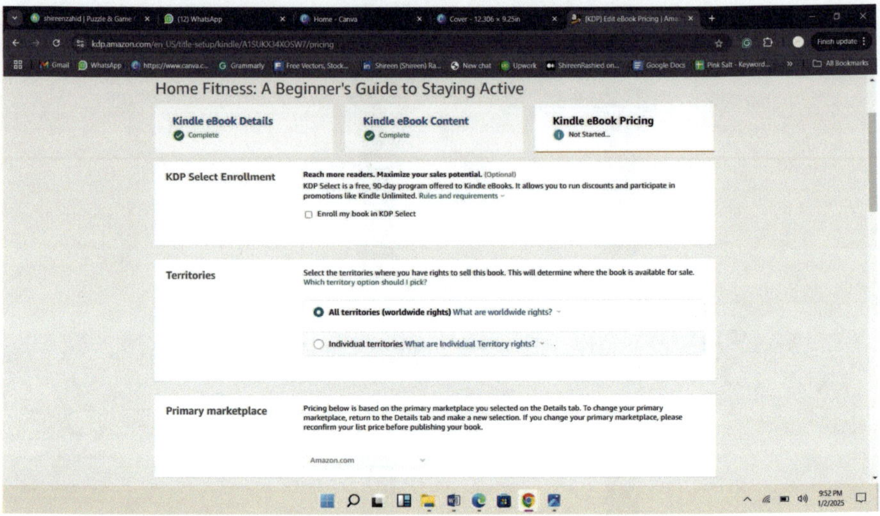

Choosing Royalties

- **Ebooks**:
    - Select between 35% and 70% royalty options. The 70% royalty option requires a minimum price of $2.99.

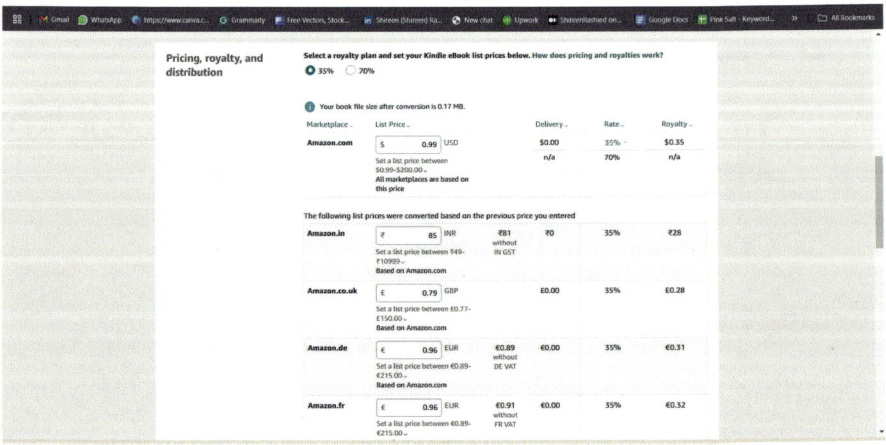

- **Paperbacks**:
    - Use Amazon's pricing calculator to determine your profit margins based on the print cost and retail price.

Setting Global Distribution

- Enable "All Territories" to make your book available worldwide.
- Adjust prices for different regions if needed.

Finalizing and Publishing

Once everything is in place, review your book details thoroughly.

- Check for typos or errors in the title, description, or keywords.
- Preview your manuscript and cover it one last time.

When you're satisfied, hit "Publish Your Book." Amazon will review your submission, and your book will typically go live within 72 hours.

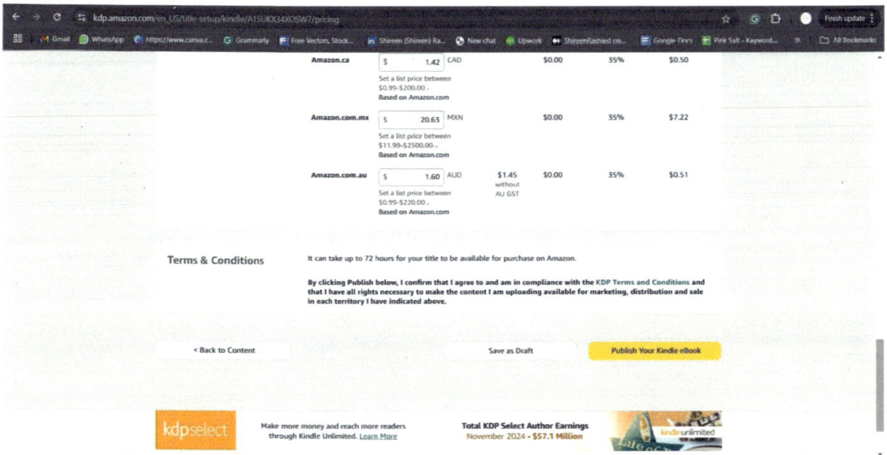

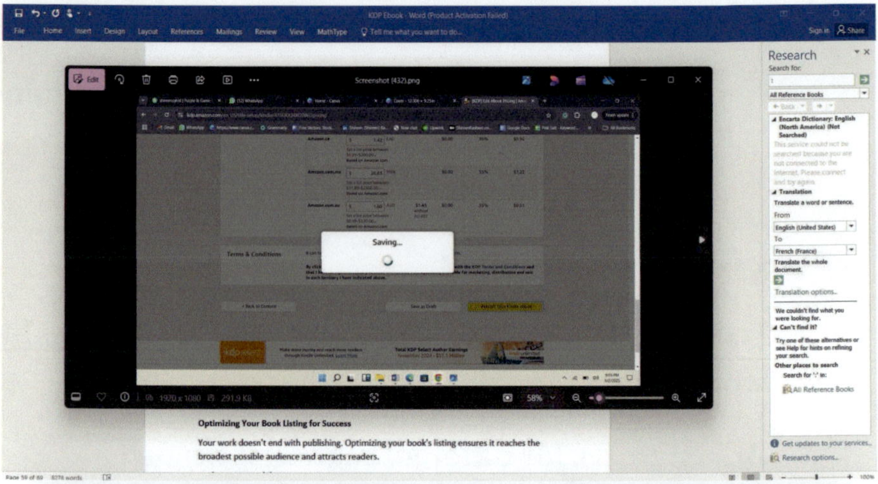

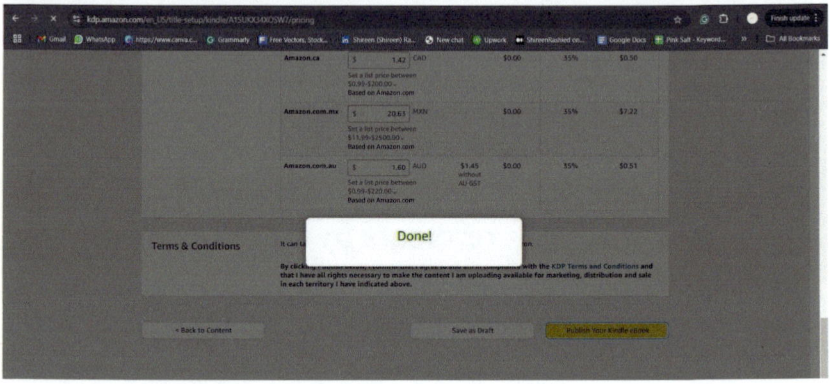

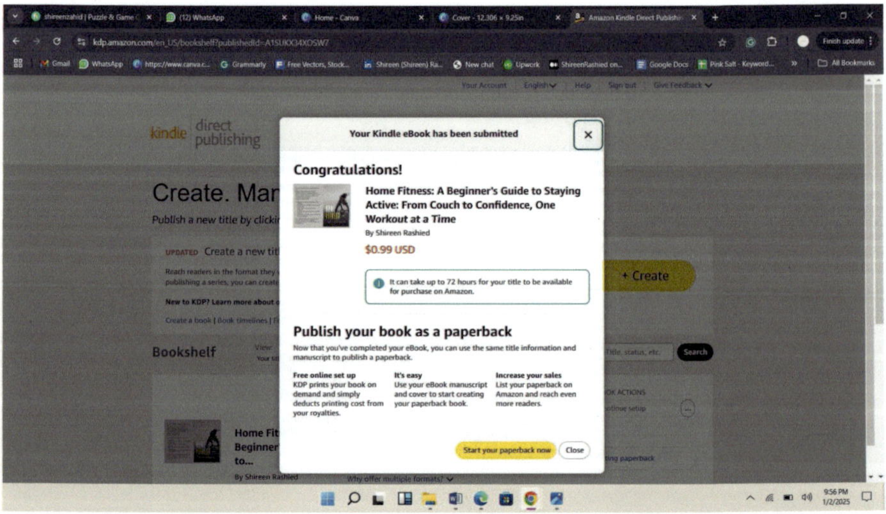

- It will be placed on the bookshelf for review.

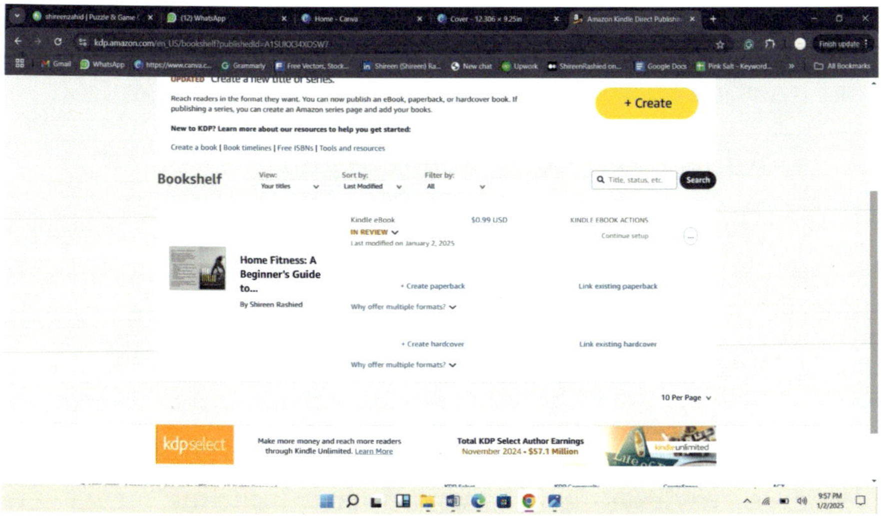

Optimizing Your Book Listing for Success

Your work doesn't end with publishing. Optimizing your book's listing ensures it reaches the broadest potential audience and attracts readers.

Crafting a Powerful Description

Make your book's description stand out by highlighting its benefits and unique features. Use bullet points for clarity and ease of reading.

Example:

- Easy-to-follow exercises for all fitness levels.
- Practical tips to build consistency and stay motivated.
- Perfect for anyone with limited time or equipment.

Creating an Author Profile

Set up your author profile on Amazon Author Central:

- ☐ Add a professional author photo.
- ☐ Write a compelling bio that reflects your expertise and passion.
- ☐ Include links to your social media or website.

Encouraging Reviews

Positive reviews are essential for building trust and credibility. Encourage readers to leave honest feedback and highlight positive reviews in your marketing.

Exercise: Publish Your Book

Take the following steps to complete the publishing process:

1. Log in to KDP and create a new title.
2. Enter all the book details, ensuring they're accurate and compelling.
3. Upload your manuscript and cover, checking for formatting issues.
4. Set your pricing and distribution preferences.
5. Preview everything and click "Publish Your Book."

Once your book is live, please share it with your network and celebrate your achievement!

Conclusion

Publishing your book on Amazon KDP is an exciting milestone. By following these steps, you've transformed your manuscript into a product ready to reach readers worldwide. The next step is promoting your book to maximise its visibility and impact. In the upcoming module, you'll explore practical strategies to market your book and connect with your audience.

Module 5

Promoting Your Book

Now comes the hard part.

Publishing your book is just the beginning. Effective promotion is essential to reach your audience and generate sales. In this module, you will explore strategies to market your book, build an engaged readership, and boost your visibility on Amazon and beyond. Whether you're new to marketing or looking to refine your approach, these techniques will help ensure your book gets the attention it deserves.

Understanding the Importance of Promotion

An outstanding book won't sell itself, especially in a competitive marketplace. Promotion helps:

- **Build Awareness**: Let readers know your book exists.
- **Generate Reviews**: Positive reviews increase trust and visibility.

- **Boost Sales**: The more your book is seen, the higher its chances of being purchased.
- **Create a Loyal Audience**: Successful marketing can turn readers into lifelong fans.

Optimizing Your Amazon Listing

The first step in promoting your book is optimizing its presence on Amazon. A well-optimised listing improves discoverability and converts browsers into buyers.

Craft a Compelling Book Description

Your description should highlight your book's value and entice readers to click the "Buy" button.

Key Elements of a Great Description:

1. Start with a hook that grabs attention.
2. Highlight the book's benefits and unique features.
3. Use bullet points to break up information and make it easier to read.
4. End with a call-to-action, such as "Get your copy today and start your journey!"

Leverage Keywords

Include relevant keywords in your book's title, subtitle, and description. Use phrases that your target audience is likely to search for. Examples include:

- For a fitness book: "home workouts," "fitness for beginners," "exercise without equipment."

Use Amazon Categories Strategically

Choose categories that align with your book's content but are moderately competitive. Research similar books to find niche categories where your book can stand out.

Add A+ Content

Amazon's A+ Content feature lets you add enhanced visuals and marketing materials to your book's listing. Use this feature to include:

- Comparison charts
- Author insights
- High-quality images and infographics

Building Your Online Presence

An active online presence helps you connect with readers and expand your reach. Here are key platforms and strategies:

Social Media

- **Choose the Right Platforms**: Focus on platforms where your target audience spends time. For Example, Instagram and Pinterest work well for visually appealing books, while LinkedIn is ideal for professional topics.
- **Post Consistently**: Share engaging content related to your book, such as tips, behind-the-scenes updates, or quotes.

- **Engage with Your Audience**: Respond to comments and messages to build a community around your book.

- **Create Shareable Content**: Use AI tools to design eye-catching graphics or short videos that highlight key aspects of your book.

Author Website

Create a professional website that showcases your book and your expertise. Include:

- A dedicated landing page for your book
- An "About the Author," section
- A blog with relevant content
- Links to purchase your book
- Testimonials or reviews from early readers

Email Marketing

Build an email list by offering free resources, such as a downloadable chapter or fitness checklist. Use this list to:

- Announce your book launch
- Share updates and exclusive content
- Encourage reviews and feedback
- Promote special discounts or promotions

Leveraging Amazon Marketing Tools

Amazon offers several advertising options to help authors promote their books directly to potential readers.

Sponsored Product Ads

- Appear in search results and product pages.
- Target specific keywords or similar books to attract the right audience.
- Set a budget and monitor a performance to maximise ROI.

Lock Screen Ads

- Display ads on Kindle devices and apps.
- Use eye-catching visuals and short, compelling text to capture attention.

Discounts and Promotions

- Offer limited-time discounts or free promotions to boost downloads and reviews.
- Enroll your book in Kindle Unlimited or KDP Select to reach a broader audience.

Collaborating with Influencers and Bloggers

Working with influencers and bloggers can help you reach a wider audience and build credibility.

Find the Right Partners

- Look for influencers in your book's niche who have an engaged following.
- Reach out with a personalised message, offering a free copy of your book for a review or feature.

Host Virtual Events

- Organise a virtual book launch, Q&A session, or live reading to engage with your audience directly.
- Use platforms like Instagram Live, YouTube, or Zoom to host these events.
- Promote these events through social media and your email list.

Generating Reviews

Positive reviews are critical for building trust and increasing sales. Encourage readers to leave reviews with these strategies:

- Include a note in your book asking readers to leave a review if they enjoyed it.
- Reach out to your email list and social media followers with review requests.
- Offer free copies to advance readers for an honest feedback.
- Engage with reviewers by thanking them and addressing any constructive criticism professionally.

Exploring Additional Channels

Beyond Amazon, there are other platforms and strategies to sell and promote your book:

- **Gumroad**: Sell digital copies directly to your audience.

- **Fiverr**: Offer personalised versions or services related to your book, such as fitness plans or coaching.
- **Your Website**: Use e-commerce tools like Shopify to sell your book directly.
- **Book Clubs**: Reach out to online book clubs and forums to promote your book.

Exercise: Build Your Promotion Plan

1. Optimize your Amazon listing by refining your description and choosing strategic keywords and categories.
2. Create a social media post schedule with at least three posts per week related to your book.
3. Reach out to five influencers or bloggers in your niche to collaborate.
4. Set up an Amazon ad campaign targeting relevant keywords.
5. Develop a free resource, such as a checklist or excerpt, to build your email list.
6. Identify one additional channel (like podcasts or Gumroad) to expand your promotion efforts.

By implementing these steps, you'll build a comprehensive promotion plan that ensures your book reaches its audience.

Conclusion

Promoting your book is a dynamic process that requires consistent effort and creativity. By leveraging Amazon's tools, building an online presence, and collaborating with influencers, you can maximise your book's visibility and sales. Exploring diverse channels beyond Amazon will help you tap into new audiences and create long-term success. In the final module, you'll explore alternative publishing options to diversify your distribution and revenue streams, ensuring your book continues to make an impact.

Module 6

Exploring Alternative Publishing and Revenue Options

Publishing your book on Amazon KDP is a fantastic way to reach a global audience, but there are other options. Diversifying your publishing strategy can open up additional revenue streams and help you connect with different audiences. In this module, you'll learn about alternative platforms, direct selling methods, and strategies to maximise your book's earning potential.

Why Explore Alternative Publishing Options?

Relying solely on one platform limits your book's reach and income potential. By branching out, you can:

- **Tap Into New Audiences**: Different platforms cater to unique reader demographics.
- **Increase Revenue Streams**: Selling through multiple channels reduces dependence on a single source.

- **Gain More Control**: Direct selling lets you set pricing, keep a higher profit margin, and build closer relationships with readers.

Alternative Publishing Platforms

Several platforms complement Amazon KDP and help you reach readers in various formats and locations.

1. Smashwords

- **Overview**: Smashwords distributes ebooks to multiple retailers, including Apple Books, Barnes & Noble, and Kobo.
- **Benefits**: One upload gives access to a broad network of retailers.
- **Best For**: Authors looking to reach non-Amazon readers and sell internationally.

2. Draft2Digital

- **Overview**: Similar to Smashwords, Draft2Digital simplifies distributing ebooks across multiple platforms.
- **Benefits**: Offers professional formatting tools and robust customer support.
- **Best For**: Authors seeking an easy, user-friendly experience.

3. IngramSpark

- **Overview**: IngramSpark specialises in distributing print books to bookstores, libraries, and online retailers.

- **Benefits**: Access to a global distribution network for paperbacks and hardcovers.
- **Best For**: Authors aiming to get their physical books into bookstores and libraries.

4. Google Play Books

- **Overview**: Google's ebook platform allows you to sell directly to Android users.
- **Benefits**: Offers unique pricing flexibility and access to a global audience.
- **Best For**: Authors focusing on digital content and Android markets.

Direct Selling Options

Selling your book directly to readers gives you complete control over pricing, branding, and audience engagement. Here are some popular methods:

1. Your Website

- **Setup**: Use platforms like WordPress or Squarespace to create a professional website with e-commerce capabilities.
- **Benefits**: Keep 100% of the profits, minus payment processing fees.
- **Best Practices**:
    - Create a dedicated landing page for your book.

    - Offer bonuses like downloadable worksheets, exclusive chapters, or video content to entice buyers.
    - Use SEO strategies to attract organic traffic.

2. Gumroad

- **Overview**: Gumroad is an easy-to-use platform for selling digital products, including ebooks.
- **Benefits**: Low transaction fees and built-in marketing tools.
- **Best Practices**:
    - Offer tiered pricing or bundles (e.g., an ebook with an accompanying video series).
    - Use Gumroad's email marketing features to stay connected with customers.

Selling Through Fiverr and Other Freelance Platforms

Freelance platforms like Fiverr can be used creatively to market your book. Instead of selling the book directly, you can package it with complementary services.

Examples of Fiverr Offerings:

- Personalised fitness plans (for a fitness book).
- Writing consultations (for a guide on writing).
- Exclusive book content or autographed copies.

Exploring Other Niches

Expanding your writing into new genres can help you reach broader audiences and develop a versatile portfolio. AI tools are excellent for brainstorming niche ideas and outlining content.

Examples of Book Genres and Prompts

- **Children's Books**:
  - Example Prompt: *"Write a story outline about teamwork for kids aged 7-10."*
- **Self-Help**:
  - Example Prompt: *"Generate 10 chapter ideas for a book on building confidence."*
- **Fiction**:
  - Example Prompt: *"Outline a mystery novel set in a small coastal town."*

By exploring different niches, you can identify markets that align with your interests and target specific demographics effectively.

Scaling Your Publishing Journey

Once you've published one book, you can scale your efforts to maximise impact and revenue. Consider these strategies:

1. Creating a Series

- Build a series of books within a niche to keep readers engaged and coming back for more. For Example, if you wrote a beginner's fitness guide, follow it up with intermediate and advanced guides.

- Use consistent branding across the series to create a cohesive identity.

2. Repurposing Content

- Turn your book into different formats, such as:
  - **Audiobooks**: Reach auditory learners by recording your book or hiring a narrator.
  - **Blog Posts**: Break your book into smaller articles for your website or guest posts.
  - **YouTube Videos**: Create video content discussing key topics from your book.

3. Expanding Your Reach

- Translate your book into other languages to reach international readers.
- Collaborate with influencers in different niches to cross-promote your work.

Maximizing Revenue Through Bundling and Upselling

Bundling and upselling strategies encourage readers to purchase more and increase the value of each sale.

Examples of Bundling:

- Offer an ebook and audiobook package.
- Include bonus materials like a workbook, cheat sheets, or video tutorials.

Upselling Opportunities:

- Provide personalised services, such as coaching or consulting, related to your book's topic.
- Offer a premium edition of your book with additional content or signed copies.

Exercise: Explore Alternative Options

1. Choose one alternative publishing platform and set up an account.
2. List your book on that platform, ensuring it meets its formatting requirements.
3. Develop a direct selling strategy using your website, Gumroad, or Patreon.
4. Create a bundle or upselling offer to maximise revenue.
5. Research local bookstores and libraries to pitch your book for inclusion.

Conclusion

Exploring alternative publishing and revenue options ensures you're independent of many platforms. By diversifying your distribution channels and leveraging creative selling strategies, you can reach new audiences, build a loyal reader base, and increase your income. With a comprehensive approach, your book's success can extend far beyond its initial release, creating lasting value for you and your readers.

Exercise: Brainstorm and Outline Your Next Book Idea

1. Choose a new genre you've never written in before, such as children's books, self-help, or fiction.
2. Use an AI tool to generate prompts and chapter ideas for this genre.
3. Create a detailed outline for your next book.
4. Plan how you can repurpose this book into other formats or expand it into a series.

By completing this exercise, you'll have a solid foundation to scale your publishing journey.

About the Author

José F. Nodar

Flung into one of life's biggest challenges at just eleven, José's story began in Havana, Cuba. The Cuban revolution forced him onto a plane alone, landing him at an orphanage in a small Georgia town called Washington. Reuniting with his parents wouldn't happen until he was eighteen, a high school graduate in Atlanta.

Business Administration became his focus at Georgia State University. From there, he navigated the world of finance, first at the First National Bank of Atlanta (now Wells Fargo) and later as a project manager in financial consulting. These roles took him across the United States, Europe, and even Australia.

It was in Camden, New South Wales, Australia, that a spark ignited José's creative side. A writers' group became the launching pad for his debut novel, and soon, his mind birthed Danny Monk, his first major character.

Currently, José is a prolific writer, working on his seventh short story collection alongside a new crime novel slated for release in 2026.

But José's life isn't all about writing. When he's not crafting captivating stories, you might find him at the local mall, observing the world and gathering inspiration for future characters. Away from his computer, he dives into books or enjoys long, leisurely walks with his wife Miriam around Camden.

Made in the USA
Monee, IL
05 November 2026

67387482R00057